The politics of poverty

POLITICS TODAY

General Editors: *Bernard Crick, Patrick Seyd*

THE POLITICS OF NATIONALISM AND DEVOLUTION   *H.M. Drucker and Gordon Brown*
THE POLITICS OF POVERTY   *Susanne MacGregor*

Forthcoming:

THE POLITICS OF LOCAL AND REGIONAL GOVERNMENT
  Alan Alexander
THE POLITICS OF WOMEN'S RIGHTS   *April Carter*
THE POLITICS OF TOWN PLANNING   *Gordon Cherry*
THE POLITICS OF THE INNER CITIES   *Geoffrey Green*
THE POLITICS OF SEXUAL MORALITY   *Cate Haste*
THE POLITICS OF PENAL REFORM   *Mick Ryan*
THE POLITICS OF ENERGY   *Roger Williams*
THE POLITICS OF TRANSPORT   *Enid Wistrich*
THE POLITICS OF LAW AND ORDER   *Michael Zander*

POLITICAL ISSUES IN MODERN BRITAIN
Published by Fontana

THE POLITICS OF THE JUDICIARY   *J.A.G. Griffith*
THE POLITICS OF EDUCATIONAL CHANGE   *Maurice Kogan*
THE POLITICS OF ECONOMIC PLANNING   *Alan Budd*
THE POLITICS OF THE MEDIA   *John Whale*
THE POLITICS OF INDUSTRIAL RELATIONS   *Colin Crouch*

THE POLITICS OF POVERTY

Susanne MacGregor

LONGMAN
London and New York

LONGMAN GROUP LIMITED
Longman House
Burnt Mill, Harlow, Essex, UK

*Published in the United States of America by Longman
Inc., New York*

© Longman Group Limited 1981

First published 1981

British Library Cataloguing in Publication Data

MacGregor, Susanne
    The politics of poverty. — (Politics today)
    1. Poverty — Political aspects
    I. Title   II. Series
    305.5'6   HC79.P6   80-42057

    ISBN 0-582-29524-6

Printed in Singapore by Huntsmen Offset Printing Pte Ltd

CONTENTS

EDITORS' PREFACE

There is a demand among the general public as well as from students for books that deal with the main issues of modern British politics in such a way that the reader can gain a reliable account of how an issue arose, of its institutional context and then, but only then, to have argument about what should be done.

Behind what have become political issues, there are fundamental problems. Many books identify these problems theoretically, but too often ignore the empirical context, and others are so polemical and doctrinaire, that their conclusions, however just, are distrusted by shrewd readers. We believe in casting out neither facts nor values, but in relating them closely but distinctly. The test of a good book on political issues should be that a reader will feel that he has a full and reliable account of how the issue arose and what institutions and groups affect and are affected by it, irrespective of what the author thinks should be done. But authors cannot just describe, inevitably they prescribe; so let it be done openly and clearly. Politics is too important for neutrality, but therefore demanding of objectivity. So we ask the authors in this series to organise the books into three parts: the recent history of the matter, the institutional setting, and argument about the future.

We believe that relevant books are wanted, neither wholly committed books nor those that pretend to scientific objectivity. This series continues work that we began with Fontana Books, in their 'Political Issues' series. Some similarities will be obvious, particularly in our injunction to authors to write at the highest possible level of intelligence but to eschew all jargon and technicalities. Students of politics should accept, not worry, that they have a public role.

Bernard Crick and Patrick Seyd

AUTHOR'S PREFACE

My aim in this book is to bring together for the general reader a range of information and comment that is usually divided between a number of different disciplines. One reason why the poor have been neglected in post-war years is that a clear perspective on this issue has been hindered by the fragmentation of the social sciences. My first debt therefore is to the many writers and researchers on whose work I have drawn liberally and, I hope, without distortion. One of the Editors, Bernard Crick, with whom I am fortunate to work at Birkbeck College, encouraged me to write this book. His perceptive comments and experienced guidance have been invaluable. I should like to thank Hugh Davies who gave expert advice and information. Tony Cutler read an early draft of the manuscript and offered useful criticism. Geoff Wood gave careful assistance in checking references and sources. I am particularly grateful to Pat Culshaw who typed the manuscript more than once with her characteristic skill and made helpful comments. Audrey Coppard, Rosemary Allen and Carol Edwards have also helped with typing. The moral support of friends and relatives who put up with my pre-occupation for many long months was very important: I should thank especially Bob Hawkins and my sons, Greg Wood and Tristan Wood. Finally, I should like to dedicate this book to my father, George White, to express my respect and gratitude to my parents.

Susanne MacGregor

ACKNOWLEDGEMENTS

We are indebted to the following for permission to reproduce copyright material:

Cambridge University Press for our table 1 from a *National Institute of Economic and Social Research* Occasional Paper 'Poverty And Progress in Britain, 1953–1973' by Fiegehen, Lansley and Smith, published by Cambridge University Press.

Part one
ORIGINS AND CONTEXT

Chapter one
THE FOUNDING OF THE WELFARE STATE

It was once believed that a 'Welfare State' was uniquely established in Britain in the 1940s. Was this the flowering of humanitarian ideals? Or the result of many years' struggle by the Labour movement? Or the product of war and the 'Dunkirk spirit'? Many historians of the forties have described a mood of popular radicalism which favoured social reform, social justice, egalitarian and collective values (Middlemas 1979; Saville 1965). But as the heady optimism waned, some questioned how real were the changes? How substantial were the reforms? It has since become fashionable to view the history of social welfare as the history of political control, denying that much was achieved in the period. Others explain these developments as a general and inevitable outcome of industrialisation and modernisation – war-time conditions in Britain may have accelerated these trends but the reforms were not crucially linked to the experience of crisis. Which of these explanations seems most satisfactory when we look at Britain in the 1940s?

The discussions and proposals of those years are especially relevant today as the return of insecurity, recession and unemployment has revived issues and debates which seemed in the days of full employment and 'Butskellism' to have been solved.

THE CONDITIONS FOR REFORM

In the early 1940s there existed a national consensus on issues of social reform (Harris 1975). Titmuss, in his *Problems of Social Policy* (1971), concluded that there was an increase both in social solidarity and of introspection on the nature of social justice, leading to pressure for social reform. What social conditions produced this mood? What created the post-war legislation often described as 'the establishment of the Welfare State'?

The poverty and hardship experienced in the 1930s and especially the administration of the Household Means Test had left a
scar on working-class memory. The unfulfilled hopes of reform
after the First World War created a determination that these failures would not be repeated.

Most accounts of the period also emphasise the significance of
the experience of war (Marwick 1970). The blots on the face of
British society were revealed. The population movements set off by
the evacuation policy and the transfer of patients under the
Emergency Hospitals programmes made people aware of inequalities in social provision. Much was made of the slum children,
their bad habits, incontinence and poor clothing, seen partly as due
to the incompetence of their mothers. At the same time, however,
the social conditions in which they lived were seen as contributing
to the problem.

Probably of more importance was the desire to win the support
of organised labour, to maintain the war effort and win the war.
The official historians of the war economy concluded: 'there
existed, so to speak, an implied contract between government and
people; the people refused none of the sacrifices that the government demanded from them for winning the war; in return, they
expected that the government should use imagination and serious-
ness in preparing for the restoration and improvement of the
nation's well-being when the war had been won.' (Hancock and
Gowing 1949: 541) This is the classical formulation of the political
contract. An alternative view stresses that material factors mattered
more than ideals. Keith Middlemas, in a recent and important
book, quotes the Head of the Ministry of Information's Home
Intelligence, Stephen Taylor, as saying at the time, 'the public is
unimaginative. It is unable, and has apparently no great wish, to
picture the details of the post-war world. It speculates relatively
little about the end of the war.' (Middlemas 1979: 275) The crucial
fact was that, during the war years, labour was a scarce commodity.
The collaboration of labour was essential. Reform of social conditions was the reward offered to trade unions and the Labour Party
for active participation in the war effort.

Deliberate attempts were also made to foster morale in the
armed forces. A new society would be the reward for sacrifice. Sol-
diers were thought to fight better 'if they believe that the stakes are
high, that freedom, justice, civilisation itself are threatened'.
(Walzer 1971: 3–4) But such propaganda really had little effect
(Taylor 1979). Of equal, if not greater, importance was the expan-

sion of the Army Education Corps. Large numbers of radical teachers conducted discussions among the troops, discussions containing a strong dose of criticism of the society which had created the war. The Army Bureau of Current Affairs, and army education in general, was a 'double-edged weapon', fostering public morale but also popular radicalism (Middlemas 1979: 360).

Equally important was the war-time expansion in spheres of State control and economic management which set precedents for peace-time social administration. 'If for warfare, why not for welfare?' Social engineering had proved practicable. Institutional changes had been effected which facilitated the administrative reforms necessary for the implementation of welfare policies. And, as José Harris, an eminent historian of British social policy, notes, because of the war-time planned economy, for the first time for thirty years the relief of poverty rather than the reduction of unemployment became the major problem and first priority of social reform (Harris 1975). The reduction of unemployment from 1 million to 100,000 by 1943 demonstrated the feasibility of a full employment policy. Full employment in itself increased Labour's bargaining power. Trade union membership increased from 6 million in 1938 to 8 million in 1944. Wage rates and earnings rose: average weekly earnings rose by 80 per cent between October 1938 and July 1945, compared to a rise in the cost of living of 31 per cent in the same period. The interests of labour were placed higher on the political agenda. At the same time such rises in the cost of living and in average earnings exacerbated the problems of low wage-earners, those on fixed benefits and with large families, the groups whose problems had been highlighted in the surveys of the 1930s. Thus the elimination of want was both manageable and desirable.

A further precondition for social reform was the increased confidence, activity and participation of representatives of the Labour movement. The role of the Labour Party in the Coalition Government and the involvement of trade unions in labour and manpower policy, being represented on the National Joint Advisory Council set up to advise the Minister of Labour, gave the working class a voice in decision-making and credence to the ability of Labour to govern.

Together, then, constant pressure by backbench MPs, army education, and the publicity given by sections of the mass media (*The Times*, *Daily Mirror*, and radio broadcasts) encouraged a mood of public opinion which supported radical social reform. It was important also that policies had been worked out in advance. The

Labour Party's deliberations of the twenties on social policy were available as a basis for discussion and their war-time proposals went well beyond anything officially sponsored by the Government (Harris 1975). Additionally, conferences of economists and political scientists, social reformers and planners (largely in the tradition of the Webbs), offered influential policy recommendations. As Keith Middlemas notes: 'Reconstruction plans usually attributed to the master designs of Beveridge and Keynes in fact owed much to the sedimentary intellectual deposits of academics, journalists and editors and bodies like the Oxford Institute of Statistics and the National Institute of Social and Economic Research.' (Middlemas 1979: 272)

Clearly social reform would serve the interests of the working class and the poor. But it would also promote the interests of the middle class and the rulers. The conscience of the middle class had been stirred. The air-raid shelters, the evacuation of children, civil defence and military service had thrown the classes together in mutual collaboration and into an intense recognition of material differences. The rulers moreover required active collaboration for national survival, not just passive obedience. Reform was the price to be paid for sacrifice and willing cooperation. Welfare became a priority on the political agenda and seemed a practicable proposition since thought had been given to the planning of policies and their implementation was demonstrably possible, as evidenced in the collective and national institutions established through war-time planning and the expansion of State control. Civil servants indeed, who before the war had doubted the feasibility of planning, found themselves planning, reasonably efficiently. Finally and crucially, the Right wing suspended its opposition. In war-time, the Conservative Party, under Churchill's leadership, defined military strategy as the dominant goal and played down domestic policies, discussion of which might encourage divisions within the Coalition Government. Such suspension of opposition was a vital ingredient in the relatively rapid advance of welfare policies in these years.

WAR-TIME SOCIAL LEGISLATION

The years 1940–41 have been seen as a dividing line in British social policy, partly due to the formation of the Coalition Government in May 1940. The increase in the cost of living had caused grave hardship to those on fixed incomes and old-age pensions and to those receiving allowances from the Unemployment Assistance

Board. In 1940, supplementary pensions were offered by the Assistance Board. Legislation, the Determination of Needs Act 1941, abolished the hated Household Means Test and transferred responsibility for provision for the very poor from the family to the community. In July 1940, Treasury aid was granted for the supply of milk to mothers and babies. In 1941, this milk scheme was followed by one for vitamin foods and later for orange juice, cod-liver oil and vitamin tablets. The same year, the Treasury aided the provision of school milk and meals, not only to those in financial need but to all school-children at reduced cost and without discrimination. This expansion of provision geared to the needs of children and the survival of the nation encouraged a positive attitude to public provision and removed the stigma which had formerly attached to the receipt of benefits in kind.

Particularly important was the evacuation scheme for mothers and children. Instituted after Munich, on a voluntary basis, 1.5 million children and mothers were involved at the time. 'For all that it was a muddled failure, the first evacuation scheme took many middle-class families a further stage along the social exploration that had been a characteristic of the thirties.' (Marwick 1970: 266) This invasion of slum children, followed by another during the Blitz of 1940, was seen as 'the most important subject in the social history of the war because it revealed to the whole people the black spots in its social life' (*The Economist*, 1 May 1943).

Concern for the children and the 'future of the race' also led an all-party deputation of MPs in 1941 to induce the Government to draw up a memorandum on Family Allowances. This was produced in May 1942.

THE BEVERIDGE REPORT

The most important war-time events to affect social policy were the setting up of the Beveridge Committee and the Report which quickly followed, events influenced partly by the need to offer a bargain to the trade unions in return for wage restraint, and partly by accident. Workmen's compensation had been the subject of a Royal Commission between 1938 and 1941. The trade unions were claiming increased benefits for industrial diseases and accidents and clashed with the employers in demanding that the whole of any increase in benefit should be paid by the latter, who in turn argued that industrial disease should not be seen as a separate problem but should be included in the contributory national health insurance scheme set up by Lloyd George in 1911. The difference between them reflected different opinions on responsibility, as the trade unions saw occupational hazards as the result of the employers' use of unsafe methods of production. More importantly, rates of benefit under national health insurance were much lower than those for workmen's compensation (Harris 1975). Little progress was achieved by the Royal Commission because of these opposed positions. A TUC deputation to the Minister of Health encouraged him to institute a review of social security policy. Ernest Bevin, the leader of the TGWU and war-time Minister of Labour, then seized the opportunity to get rid of the unpopular Beveridge (the former Director of the London School of Economics) and pushed him out of the Ministry of Labour and onto the Committee. So it was that the Minister without Portfolio, Arthur Greenwood, also a trade unionist, announced the appointment of Sir William Beveridge as chairman of the Committee on Social Insurance and Allied Services on 10 June 1941. The Committee's terms of reference were limited:

To undertake with special reference to the inter-relation of the schemes, a survey of the existing national schemes of social insurance and allied services, including workmen's compensation, and to make recommendations.

A review of social security provision was indeed urgently required. There were wide variations in the extent, duration and coverage of benefits under different types of social insurance and assistance. In 1940, the General Council of the TUC had concluded that what was necessary was the complete overhauling of the whole scheme of national health insurance and the related social services. Their deputation to the Minister of Health in February 1941 had stressed the importance of the coordination and integration of schemes, the need for a comprehensive plan. Thus from the spring of 1941, pressure had built up from within the Home Office and the Ministry of Health to establish a social insurance committee which would, it was hoped, expose the anomalies of the existing system. Bevin, in supporting the Committee, was keen to emphasise, however, that it should not be a 'policy enquiry', but should be concerned with technical questions of social administration. This was a quite unrealistic hope since the deliberations of the Committee were seen by his contemporaries as evidence of a conscious attempt by the war-time Government to abolish poverty, as one of the essentials for pursuing the national war effort and as a blueprint for freedom from want (Harris 1975).

José Harris, who has devoted particular attention to the study of British social policy in this period, emphasises three points in her conclusions: first, the Beveridge plans should not be seen as an expression of the aims and ideals of the war-time Coalition Government; second, Beveridge himself contributed little that was intrinsically original to the discussion of plans for social reconstruction; and third, the significance of the Report lies in its synthesis of secondary opinions and transmission to a popular audience of ideas which had long been in vogue among journalists, academics, trade unionists and public administrators (ibid.).

More radical contemporary views were expressed by G.D.H. Cole writing in 1942. He argued for the 'right to work' or for decent maintenance if work was not to be had. The experiences of the 1930s, where 'just and unjust' alike were confronted by a drastic fall in their standard of living, had given a new intensity to the claim for security. Cole linked the desire for social security with those for a minimum wage, family allowances and a full employment policy. 'Social security' more widely interpreted referred to the certainty of a minimum standard of real income for everyone prepared to work or prevented from doing so by youth, age or any sort of incapacity. Cole emphasised the important and direct link between the need for a minimum wage policy and adequate social security provision. 'Wages in the worst-paid occupations are so low that the guarantee of a tolerable income to the unemployed or sick who belong to these grades of labour is bound to mean paying them more than they can earn when they are at work, at all events when there are dependent children or adults to be cared for.' (Cole 1942: 139) These comments by Cole, and the principles and assumptions of the Beveridge Plan, express arguments and opinions clearly of relevance today.

The appointment of the arrogant and energetic Beveridge, not a Socialist incidentally but a Liberal, was crucial in transforming the social insurance enquiry from a 'machinery of government' exercise to one of 'high policy'. The Report was produced in draft form in the summer of 1942, barely twelve months after the Committee had been called into being. This draft was considered to be so outrageous that the civil servants on the Committee were not allowed to sign it and were downgraded from being full members to being merely 'advisors and assessors' lest the proposals should be thought to represent the official views of the respective Government departments (Harris 1975).

The Report, submitted on 20 November 1942, was accordingly

signed by W.H. Beveridge alone and entitled *Social Insurance and Allied Services: Report by Sir William Beveridge*. It was divided into six parts: Part I, Introduction and Summary; Part II, The Principal Changes Proposed and their Reasons; Part III, Three Special Problems; Part IV, The Social Security Budget; Part V, Plan for Social Security; and Part VI, Social Security and Social Policy. It also contained seven appendices. The first duty placed on the Committee had been to survey; the second, to recommend. The Survey, however, formed only a small part of the Report. It concluded that the schemes existing at the time had grown piecemeal and with little reference to each other. The existing services, excluding medical care, were considered comparable with those of any other country, but the duplication of effort involved in their administration by several different departments and institutions proceeding on different principles was inefficient. The variation in coverage and rates of benefit was illogical and produced an incoherent system. 'It is not open to question that by closer co-ordination, the existing services could be made at once more beneficial and more intelligible to those whom they serve and more economical in their administration.' (Beveridge Report: para. 5)

The 'Three Guiding Principles' of the Recommendations appeared early in the Report and have attained deserved fame. Solemnly capitalised, they demonstrate the resounding Pilgrim's Progress tone of the Report which had much to do with its impact:

The first principle is that any proposals for the future, while they should use to the full the experience gathered in the past, should not be restricted by consideration of sectional interests established in the obtaining of that experience. Now, when the war is abolishing landmarks of every kind, is the opportunity for using experience in a clear field. A revolutionary moment in the world's history is a time for revolutions, not for patching.

The second principle is that organisation of social insurance should be treated as one part only of a comprehensive policy of social progress. Social insurance fully developed may provide income security; it is an attack upon Want. But Want is one only of five giants on the road of reconstruction and in some ways the easiest to attack. The others are Disease, Ignorance, Squalor and Idleness.

The third principle is that social security must be achieved by co-operation between the State and the individual. The State should offer security for service and contribution. The State in organising security should not stifle incentive, opportunity, responsibility; in establishing a national minimum, it should leave room and encouragement for voluntary action by each individual to provide more than that minimum for himself and his family. (op. cit.: paras. 7–9)

The Plan for Social Security was proposed as a limited contribution to social policy: 'It is first and foremost a plan of insurance – of giving in return for contributions, benefits up to subsistence level, as of right and without means test, so that individuals may build freely upon it.' (op. cit.: para.10)

The Plan 'starts from a diagnosis of want – of the circumstances in which, in the years just preceding the present war, families and individuals in Britain might lack the means of healthy subsistence' (op. cit.: para. 11). It accepted the findings of the surveys of the 1930s which had shown that 'want' or poverty was caused by interruption or loss of earning-power in over three-quarters of the cases examined. The remaining main cause of poverty was 'failure to relate income earning to the size of the family' that is, as we would say today, low wages plus the demands made by children: 'abolition of want requires a double redistribution of income, through social insurance and by family needs'. (op. cit: para. 11) These conclusions and policy proposals remain central to discussions of poverty today. What seemed to Beveridge to be self-evident commonsense, not a matter for political dispute, has still not gained universal acceptance either in principle or practice.

Beveridge noted that most of the causes of poverty were already covered by schemes of social insurance. That poverty remained in spite of these provisions resulted from the fact that 'the benefits amount to less than subsistence', as measured by the standards adopted in the social surveys, 'or do not last as long as the need, and that the assistance which supplements insurance is either insufficient in amount or available only on terms which make men unwilling to have recourse to it'. The remedies lay therefore in three directions, 'by extension of scope to cover persons now excluded; by extension of purposes to cover risks now excluded; and by raising the rates of benefits' (op. cit.: para. 12).

Beveridge also proposed measures to meet family needs, that is allowances for children. He aimed to abolish poverty through a redistribution of income through social insurance and children's allowances. The main method should be compulsory social insurance with national assistance and voluntary insurance as subsidiary methods. 'It assumes allowances for children as part of its background. The Plan assumes also the establishment of comprehensive health and rehabilitation services and maintenance of employment, that is to say, avoidance of mass unemployment, as necessary conditions of success in social insurance.' (op. cit.: para. 14)

The Plan was based on a diagnosis of want and was aimed at its abolition. It had two other intentions: the requirement to take account of the increasing proportion of old people in the population and the 'urgent' need to increase the birth-rate.

The six fundamental principles of the Plan for Social Security were: flat rate of subsistence benefit; flat rate of contribution; unification of administrative responsibility; adequacy of benefit; comprehensiveness; and classification (op. cit.: para. 17). These six principles were viewed as inviolable. The rest of the proposals were suggestions put forward as a basis for constructive discussions and seen as open to amendment.

What was so significant about Beveridge's Plan was his assumption that any reconstruction of social security must take place within a context of full employment, universal medical care and the payment of family allowances at subsistence level. The emphasis on benefits fixed at subsistence level was crucial to the entire plan. Uniform benefits payable at subsistence rates should be given for all interruptions of earnings to all insured persons, who would include not only the working class but the whole employed and self-employed population. The principles of universalism, collectivism and subsistence rates were central. However, it was a plan for *insurance* and was intended to be self-financing through a redistribution of national income. It had therefore to be a long-term plan. Full rates of benefit would be reached only gradually. Old-age pensions, a crucial item in the integrated system, would not be payable at the full rates for 20 years. After these 20 years, however, which would have been in about 1966, British society would see the end of the Poor Law and an end to supplementation. It was this panoramic vision of future social policy that lifted the Beveridge Report above run-of-the-mill Committee Reports and ensured it a place in the history of British social administration (Harris 1975); and this perspective was largely Beveridge's own, not shared by the civil servants who sat with him on the Committee. He insisted on seeing social security as part of a much wider spectrum of economic and social reform. His proposals, with their important assumptions, were statements not only about the need for an internally linked and consistent system of social security, but of the need to tie social security to other key policies to establish the fabric of a 'Welfare State': policies for health, education, full employment, housing and planning.

Beveridge condensed and integrated the common attitudes of those who gave evidence to his Committee. He put forward a logical, rational plan based on what he perceived to be the consensus of values and attitudes necessary to ensure the cooperation of the people in the scheme. The six main policy proposals, family allowances, maintenance of full employment, a universal free national health service, uniform system of contributory insurance, subsistence level benefits and the final abolition of poor relief, were views which were almost universally popular.

If it had not been for the existence by 1942–3 of widespread popular radicalism, focused directly on programmes of reform for the first time since the mid-1920s (and perhaps since the age of the Chartists) which the Labour Party utilised and the Conservatives could not ignore, then government might have relegated Beveridge and his Report to a rosy but indefinite future. (Middlemas 1979: 273)

Family allowances had in fact been accepted in principle by the Coalition Government before Beveridge's Report was submitted. Beveridge supported them as a means of promoting population growth and as a device to protect the differential between subsistence level insurance benefits and the income of low paid workers. Full employment was viewed as essential for the financial viability of the scheme. Exactly what 'full employment' meant to Beveridge is difficult to assess – his estimates varied between 2½ per cent and 8 per cent of the registered labour force. But he believed in a pragmatic way that a Government that could abolish unemployment in war-time could do so in times of peace.

Flat-rate benefits have often been criticised, generally because they have been fixed at a low rate. Beveridge seems never to have seriously considered a graduated scheme, but his rate was based firmly on the principle of a *subsistence* minimum. This was a constructively original aspect of the Beveridge Report, a striking departure from Lloyd George's view of national insurance as merely a foundation for voluntary private saving (Harris 1975). It is interesting to note Harris' comment that Beveridge did not view subsistence as a scientifically immutable concept, but as one that could be adjusted to the changing communal standard of living.

The Coalition Government was hoist by its own petard in its handling of the Beveridge Committee. Churchill believed firmly that no commitment should be made to social reform until after the restoration of peace, but constant pressure from backbench MPs forced the Government to make some response. They pointed to the existence of the Beveridge Committee and the need to await its findings to stave off demands for action, but this postponement of decisions on family allowances, increased rates of benefit and extended medical care created the impression that Ministers would accept the proposals of the Committee. The Report was also seized upon by the Ministry of Information and used for propaganda purposes, becoming a best-seller in Britain and the USA. Reactions in parliamentary and civil service circles meant that the Beveridge Report could neither be ignored nor suppressed. However, the ambivalence and hostility to the Report which also existed must temper any easy conclusion about a 'national consensus' on issues of social reform.

That there were differences of opinion is clear from the submissions of expert witnesses to the social insurance committee. The Friendly Societies, who had most to lose immediately by reform, wanted sickness insurance to continue through the voluntary associations. The industrial assurance companies hoped for a share in the administration of national insurance in order to retain, in particular, their lucrative door-to-door collections. Public Assistance officials were surprisingly outspoken in condemning the existing provision as 'inadequate, overlapping, ungenerous, and inefficient', denouncing the 'meanness of Means Tests' and calling for a dismantling of the Poor Laws (Harris 1975). The section of society whose attitudes and policy Beveridge's proposals most directly reflected and articulated were the trade unions and radical reformers. The TUC agreed with Beveridge on every major issue apart from their original claim that workmen's compensation should not be integrated with the rest of social insurance. Beveridge hoped for a compromise by offering them wider reforms in exchange for the loss of this particular policy. The trade unions' representatives to the Beveridge Committee had expressed the traditional values of the labour aristocracy: they were in favour of contributory insurance; contemptuous of 'dodgers', the 'very poor', and of 'the type of person who will not join a Friendly Society'; and, perhaps surprisingly, the leaders of the delegation favoured the withdrawal of public assistance from the wives and children of workers who went on strike.

THE RESPONSE TO BEVERIDGE AND POST-WAR LEGISLATION

A report awaited with intense interest, received favourably and so effectively publicized, demanded a response from the Government. The Phillips Committee, a committee of civil servants, was established to consider and comment on the Beveridge Report. This committee rejected the idea of subsistence benefits. To do this, they seized on a major flaw in Beveridge's proposals. While he had calculated the components and cost of a subsistence diet in minute detail, he had at the same time rather casually simply added a notional amount for rent. This was clearly inadequate, given the vast differences in rent paid in different regions, especially between London and Scotland.

This criticism was incorporated into the White Paper on *Social Insurance* of 1944 which argued against the idea of a 'national minimum': 'Benefits must be paid for and a high level of benefit must mean a high level of contribution. The Government therefore conclude that the right objective is a rate of benefit which provides a reasonable insurance against want and at the same time takes account of the maximum contribution which the great body of contributors can properly be asked to bear.' Thus the flat-rate principle emphasised by Beveridge was turned against him, and perhaps fairly, for the principles of subsistence and of flat-rate contributions and benefits are indeed incompatible.

The Phillips Committee also reduced the proposed level of family allowances and was sceptical of the possibility of maintaining full employment. Although Beveridge had deliberately put forward his proposals simply as a basis for discussion, the Phillips Committee recommended that they be either totally accepted or totally rejected. The watering down of the Report which then followed was not really surprising. The White Paper on *Social Insurance* of September 1944 was part of that flurry of activity which Beveridge named memorably the 'White Paper Chase', but right up to the time when the Churchill Government fell, in the middle of 1945, none of the Bills needed to carry these proposals into effect had been produced. This delay contrasts with the assessments of some historians who have emphasised the speed and decisiveness of social legislation in this period. Some of the delay resulted from doubts about the cost of the Beveridge plan. A fear was also voiced, which had been heard since at least 1834 and is still present today, that too much State help to the poor and the workers would undermine the incentive to labour and unduly strengthen the hands of the trade unions in wage bargaining. 'Cradle to grave' provision would reduce the spirit of adventure and enterprise and mollycoddle the people. The administrative changes necessary for the implementation of the legislation would certainly cause disturbance and aroused opposition from established interests, like the Friendly Societies and the Civil Service. For example, Beveridge had proposed a Ministry of Social Security. In the process of discussion this became firstly Social Insurance and then National Insurance. Eventually, in 1944, a Ministry of National Insurance was proposed, designed to have much narrower functions than Beveridge had envisaged.

As we have seen, children's allowances had been accepted in principle before Beveridge reported. But they were not to be at subsistence rates and thus a prime aim of Beveridge's plan, the abolition of poverty due to the costs of child-rearing, was defeated.

Beveridge was criticised from one side for the cost, extravagance and impracticality of some of his proposals. The other side welcomed his focus on want arising from unemployment, sickness, accident, old age, and the contribution of low wages together with the costs of child-rearing; but they criticised him for neglecting those cases in which men and women in work, in health and in the prime of life, could not earn a living wage; that is, for avoiding the problem of low wages. Bevin believed social security would be fostered mainly by full employment and good wage standards rather than by any 'social ambulance' scheme. His ideas about post-war reconstruction were for fuller employment, fair shares between industrial profits and wages, a Welfare State, education for all up to sixteen and 'a new conception of industrial relations beginning with better wages and conditions (to be secured by joint negotiation) and extending to something approaching a partnership on equal terms between management and workers (and) the extension of joint consultation with the unions and employees to the whole range of government economic and social policy' (Bullock 1960: 191). He went some way towards tackling the problem of low wages with the Wage Councils Act 1945. This gave the Government power to set up a wage council in any occupation in which no adequate voluntary wage-fixing machinery was in operation and in which a reasonable standard of remuneration was not maintained. These councils would have the power to fix minimum standards of remuneration, enforceable by law. Minimum wage legislation, however, was not accepted.

The acceptance of State responsibility for full employment in the White Paper of 1944 marks a critical point in the political economy of post-war Britain together with the acceptance of national income budgeting as one technique of economic management (White Paper on *National Income and Expenditure*, 1942). The establishment of the principle of Government responsibility for the economy meant that parties and Governments would increasingly be judged on their record on issues of employment and the cost of living.

The payment of family allowances to the mother marked a partial recognition of the independence of wives and children from the husband. The notion that the sins of the fathers should be visited on the children was thus partly dented, so that if he was unemployed, sick or on strike, his dependents should not be made to suffer. But Beveridge had proposed an allowance of 8 shillings. The Coalition Government's proposals of September 1944 were for a benefit of 5 shillings, with no provision made for adjustment to offset increased prices. The Government argued that more benefits in kind, school meals and milk, would be provided instead and anyway that the original Beveridge plan was too costly.

Beveridge had proposed that benefits for the sick and the unemployed be the same. These benefits should be of unlimited duration, a policy which would be supported by an increase in retraining and rehabilitation services. Benefit would be payable indefinitely, given proper medical evidence and on condition of the acceptance of a suitable job, where available, or the offer of retraining or rehabilitation where required. Training benefit should be available to all who needed it, not only to the unemployed, reflecting Beveridge's interest in manpower planning. The Coalition Government's proposals, however, dropped all provision for rehabilitation and refused to make either unemployment benefit or sickness benefit unlimited in duration. After a specified period, the recipient would have to resort to the Assistance Board, where the means test would still apply.

The Labour Government produced its National Insurance Bill in 1946. In many ways this followed the lines of the Coalition White Paper, although there were some improvements. Sickness benefits would be of unlimited duration. Unemployment benefit was limited to 180 days, with the proviso that at the discretion of local tribunals this could be extended for a further period. In this the legislation clearly fell short of the Beveridge proposals. In its Industrial Injuries Act of 1946 the Labour Government also followed the main lines of the Coalition White Paper but benefits were made more extensive and the claims of parents and dependent relatives were recognised. The Act was viewed however, as an advance on the old system of workmen's compensation, since the delay due to determination by the courts, which had been a source of complaint under the previous scheme, was avoided. Flat-rate payments were initially made, followed by a disablement pension or allowance at an increased rate when the individual's case had been assessed. Provision was made, however, only for the employed: the housewife, small employer and the independent worker would still have to resort to national assistance. The neglect of certain categories, especially that of the housewife, in Beveridge and in the post-war legislation, has produced many of the problems for social policy since, in particular the needs of the chronically sick and disabled, the young unemployed and single-parent families. (The long-term unemployed were not neglected by Beveridge but were by the post-war legislation.)

As Beveridge had pointed out, the old were a rapidly rising proportion of the population. Beveridge began with a scale of pensions admittedly inadequate, although better than the existing scales, and planned to increase gradually over twenty years the amounts paid. Although sensible as regards actuarial calculation, it would obviously be offensive politically to discriminate between age-groups in this way, virtually writing off a generation of old people. The Coalition Government proposed instead to bring in a fixed scale of pensions at once, but at rates lower than the final ones proposed by Beveridge. The low rate at which these were set, inadequate to afford a tolerable standard of living, set the scene for an endemic problem in British social policy in post-war years. The Labour Government's Act of 1946, instituted in July 1948, split the difference between the rates proposed by Beveridge and those of the Coalition Government. It also legislated for widows' pensions and lowered from 50 to 40 years the age at which widows without dependent children could receive a pension, and also instituted a death grant, which dealt a blow to the industrial assurance companies.

One key problem concerned the general level of payments. Beveridge had based his rates on a price level 25 per cent above the pre-war one. By 1944, however, prices had risen by more than 33 per cent. The Coalition Government accepted Beveridge's figures without adjustment to the higher price level and without promise of further adjustment. The Labour Government, while generally raising the rates above the White Paper levels, followed the White Paper in laying down fixed benefits without any automatic provision for varying them as the cost of living changed (indexing). A quinquennial review of the rates was established, however, 'with particular regard to any changes in the expenditure needed for the preservation of health and working capacity' (1946 National Insurance Act).

The post-war legislation rested on the investigations and planning undertaken during the war. The rates payable were raised and the subsistence principle, although not explicitly accepted, influenced decisions about rates of pay which were initially based on 1938 assessments of minimum needs plus some allowance for the increased cost of living. There was a tacit acceptance of the need to link rates of benefit with the cost of living. A vast expansion of staff was required to implement the legislation. The staff of the Ministry of National Insurance grew from 5,600 in 1945 to 40,000 in 1948. The integrated nature of services for health, insurance and assistance was formally symbolised in the choice of the same day, 5 July 1948, as the appointed date for the initiation of the National Health Service, National Insurance and National Assistance. With the setting up of the National Assistance Board, viewed as a safety-net to protect those not covered by all other provisions, the Poor Law was thought to have been formally abolished. It was claimed that the long process which had seen the growth of responsibility from the parish to the nation was complete. The local authorities, however, retained responsibility for personal welfare services.

The Labour Government's legislation was based on the principle of universality – the provision of free medical treatment, family allowances, pensions and insurance benefits to rich and poor alike – and aimed to eliminate the stigma of 'social services'. Some saw it as aiming a blow at class distinctions and saw such provision as a step to raising standards, since only when the rich shared services with the poor would the poor get the best available. 'In the context of 1945 the insistence on universality can be seen as one of the few aspects of Labour policy that do show a genuine social revolutionary intention in the sense of aiming at a substantial modification of the class basis of British society' (Marwick 1970: 345). Services were to be provided universally, without discrimination, and unified into one integrated Welfare State. This aim must now be seen as merely pious aspiration. The piece meal development surveyed by Beveridge survived in spite of the remedies he prescribed, mainly because these remedies were administered in neither the correct dose nor manner. Lack of integration and coordination have remained central features of British social security.

CONCLUSION

How significant were the 1940s for social reform? Can the period be defined as one in which the ideas of universalism, collectivism and egalitarianism flourished? If these were the dominant ideals of the age, how substantially were they embodied in social legislation and what were the social forces which underlay these policies? Which was the more important, war or the pursuit of socialism, in providing the social conditions in which these changes occurred? And, within the discussions, investigations and policies of the period, can we discern what were to become the dominant issues and problems for social policy in the post-war years, and the principles of social philosophy which have dictated ensuing debates about poverty and social welfare?

We may begin with Titmuss's assessment of the period: he emphasised the impact of war and the changes in attitudes, values, perceptions of duty and responsibility which resulted. 'By the end of the Second World War the Government had, through the agency of newly established or existing services, assumed and developed a measure of direct concern for the health and well-being of the population which, by contrast with the role of Government in the 1930s, was little short of remarkable.' (Titmuss 1971: 506) A new definition of State responsibility had been made and accepted. 'No longer did concern rest on the belief that, in respect to many social needs, it was proper to intervene only to assist the poor and those who were unable to pay for services of one kind and another. Instead, it was increasingly regarded as a proper function or even obligation of Government to ward off distress and strain among not only the poor but almost all classes of society' (ibid.). The principle of universalism was added to that of collective responsibility, abolishing social discrimination and improving standards. 'Poor Law' provision on 'a standard inflexible in administration and attuned to a philosophy which regarded individual distress as a mark of social incapacity' (ibid.) was replaced by the willingness to pool national resources and share risks.

This promotion of the goals of welfare resulted, Titmuss argued, from the needs of the war machine for more men and more work; partly by accident, and partly through the recognition of needs hitherto hidden by ignorance of social conditions. Anthony Eden had stated in the House of Commons on 6 December 1939 that war 'exposed weaknesses ruthlessly and brutally ... which called for revolutionary change in the economic and social life of the country'. Reports on the condition of evacuated mothers and children stirred the conscience of the nation. Values changed with self-criticism and national introspection promoted by war-time experience. Even *The Times* wrote in a leader of 1 July 1940:

If we speak of democracy, we do not mean a democracy which maintains the right to vote but forgets the right to work and the right to live. If we speak of freedom, we do not mean a rugged individualism which excludes social organisation and economic planning. If we speak of equality, we do not mean a political equality nullified by social and economic privilege. If we speak of economic reconstruction, we think less of maximum production (though this too will be required) than of equitable distribution.

Titmuss saw such views as being part of an impulse toward a more generous society. He stressed the unanimity underlying policy and the speed at which decisions were acted on. The universal character of these welfare policies ensured their acceptance and success; they were free of social discrimination and the inadequacies of the Poor Law. There was, he thought, a desire to remove or lessen inequalities, a conspicuous absence of direct or implied discrimination and an increase in humane treatment. A differing conception of social duty emerged. 'The area of collective responsibility moved out... drawing in more people and broadening the obligations to protect those in need.' (Titmuss 1971: 517)

This somewhat euphoric assessment is present also in Maurice Bruce's discussion. He too sees in the levelling influence of war a force for equity and egalitarian policies: A new spirit was abroad. The principle of universalism was recognised in war-time conditions: from marginal provision to the destitute and helpless, policy had developed into a pooling of national resources to see all its members through any of the ills that social care could relieve (Bruce 1968). How much, however, was rhetoric and how much substance? The White Paper on *Social Insurance* states that 'concrete expression is thus given to the solidarity and unity of the nation, which in war have been its bulwarks against aggression and in peace will be its guarantees of success in the fight against individual want and mischance'. Such phrases bear the mark of propaganda or at best 'pious aspiration'. Yet Bruce concludes:

the decisive event in the evolution of the Welfare State was the Second World War which, coming as it did after a long period of distress and puzzled endeavour at relief, challenged the British people to round off a system of social security that they had sketched and to maintain in peace the consideration for all which had so impressively marked the war period... The war speeded changes and left a country markedly different and, for all its losses, markedly more humane and civilised than that of 1939. (Bruce 1968: 326)

If principles of collective responsibility, universal provision and an expansion in the role of the State were established in the 1940s, how long were they to last? Beveridge, writing in 1953, concluded sadly 'the picture of yesterday's hopeful collaboration in curing the evils of want and disease, ignorance and squalor... looks like a dream today' (Beveridge 1953: 360–1). Yet, in retrospect, it is clear that it was collaboration not consensus that existed. Divisions of opinion remained, not only latently, and many of the principles proposed by Beveridge were neither accepted nor established, while others were eroded in the post-war years. The debates between selectivism and universalism, between individualism and collectivism, were not finally settled in the 1940s. The conflict between these principles has continued. In the 1940s, the strength of labour, economically and politically, swung the balance of forces in favour of universalism and collective responsibility. However, even the extent to which these principles were actively promoted by the representatives of Labour is in doubt. The 'battle of ideas' did not have clearly drawn lines between Labour and Conservative, or between trade unions and employers. The men at ICI, for example, Melchett and McGovern, and the 120 signatories of *A National Policy for Industry* held more paternalistic views. They argued for 'a welfare system including corporately provided employees' housing, supplements to state pensions and subsidies against unemployment' (Middlemas 1979: 287). In a poll conducted at the time, 75 per cent of employers thought the Beveridge Report should be adopted. The values of the TUC witnesses to the Beveridge Committee exemplify one strand, those of the Conservative Reform Group another, which cannot easily be fitted into a simple categorisation of Left and Right.

The Beveridge plan was not adopted *in toto*. The energy of the man, the phraseology and the promotion of the Report helped to push social welfare on to the political agenda, higher in the list of priorities, and demanded a response from Government. Combined with the pressures of backbench MPs, reformers and trade unions, social policy could not be ignored. The plan crystallised the ideas of strong pressure groups and in its emphasis on the need for coordination of services, integration, a comprehensive plan for social welfare, on the necessity to link a number of institutions and policies, it drew a picture, a blueprint, for a 'Welfare State'. As such it serves as a model by which to assess the social policy of both the war years and those that followed. Beveridge aimed to abolish poverty through the provision of subsistence benefits, adequate family allowances and the payment of benefit as long as the need were to last. None of these three key features of his plan for social security was enacted in the post-war legislation: indeed, the implementation of all three today would dramatically improve the situation of the poor. Problems following from the failure to implement the Beveridge plan in post-war years have related to the inadequacy of benefits, especially for the old and the sick, who have had to resort in increasing numbers to national assistance or supplementary benefits. Poverty among children and the existence of the 'poverty trap' have been affected by low rates of child benefit. The failure in most post-war years to regularly relate benefits to the cost of living or to increases in average earnings has periodically increased the distress of the poor. Other problems relate to issues neglected or unforeseen by Beveridge, especially the position of women and the housewife, which explain the difficulties faced by single-parent families and the chronically sick and disabled. Other problems are those of the long-term unemployed and the question of low wages, the need, that is, not only for an adequate minimum income from benefits, but also for an adequate minimum wage from work. Beveridge's emphasis, through his principles and assumptions, on the crucial inter-relationship between full employment, health, housing, social security and education, is a recognition that a narrow view of the causes of poverty and of the aims of social policy is inadequate. Social problems should be seen not as the responsibility of the individual but as a communal responsibility requiring collective action and State intervention.

Let us see how far these principles have influenced the development of social policy regarding social security and the problems of poverty and inequality in the years since he wrote.

Chapter two
SOCIETY AND SECURITY IN POST-WAR BRITAIN

On the morrow of the electoral victory of the Labour Party in the summer of 1945, nineteenth-century ideas of individualism were widely regarded as outdated as well as socially immoral. The lessons of the grim years of unemployment and wasted resources between the wars had bitten deeply into the minds and hearts of many of the British people, and the anti-fascist war had further strengthened their radicalism. There was at this time a greater consensus of opinion regarding the allocation of resources in the interests of social justice and equality than at any previous time in the twentieth century, or, for that matter, since. (John Saville 1965: 199)

The story of poverty, inequality and the Welfare State in post-war Britain is one of a retreat from that consensus on social justice and equality to which Saville refers. We have argued that what agreement there was in public opinion in the forties reflected less a fundamental shift in attitudes and allegiances than a collaboration forged from the specific situation of a nation at war, and that what was established in the late 1940s did not meet the criteria proposed by Beveridge and fell far short of those principles which define the 'Welfare State'.

A 'welfare state' is a state in which organised power is deliberately used (through politics and administration) in an effort to modify the play of market forces in at least three directions – first, by guaranteeing individuals and families a minimum income irrespective of the market value of their work or their property;' second, by narrowing the extent of 'social contingencies' (for example, sickness, old age and unemployment) which lead otherwise to individual and family crises; and third by ensuring that all citizens without distinction of status or class are offered the best standards available in relation to a certain agreed range of social services. (Briggs 1961: 288)

Other objectives of the Welfare State might be the provision of education, the maintenance of full employment, the pursuit of economic growth and the redistribution of income from rich to poor. Social policy and practice in Britain in post-war years have not been directed consistently and determinedly towards these objectives. Developments have been erratic, *ad hoc*, incoherent and even contradictory. Progress towards one goal has usually been off-set by erosion of what has been achieved on others. Viewing together the inadequacies of the post-war legislation and the direction of policies in the ensuing thirty years, Marwick commented that the 'mosaic' of social services would be better described as a 'crazy pavement' (Marwick 1967: 401). The complacent view that the problems of poverty and insecurity had been solved dominated for many years and the issues disappeared from public debate until rediscovered in the 1960s, partly influenced by similar discoveries in the United States. The contemporary history of social security and social services has been described as the 'withering away of the Welfare State' (Marwick 1970: 430). The phrase refers in part to the dismantling and undermining of the structure of social provision and its supporting values and in part to the demystification of an idea all too readily taken for granted.

The period 1950–80 saw a hardening of attitudes towards the poor, less concern for the pursuit of social justice and equality, reduced representation of these causes by Labour and a retreat from the principles of universalism and collectivism. Evidence accumulated to demonstrate the continuance of poverty, inequality and insecurity but concern for these issues remained secondary to the pursuit of economic growth and related problems of public expenditure and the level of taxation.

The issue which dominated discussion was that of the relatively low rate of economic growth achieved by Britain compared to other advanced industrial countries. The slump-boom cycle of the 1950s and 1960s, with stop-go Government policies, continued into the 1970s, which were obsessed by the phenomenon of 'stagflation', rising unemployment coinciding with high rates of inflation. 'The long-term decline of Britain', banal though that description may seem, marks the wider context within which discussion of social security must be placed.

The most striking change was in the general standard of living. Material prosperity greatly increased in post-war Britain. Sue Toland, from a survey of living standards, concluded that three changes since 1950 were particularly significant. Opportunities for young people had broadened; women (and mothers in particular) were more likely to have paid jobs, and people worked fewer hours and had longer holidays. Using constant 1975 prices, average earn-ings for a male manual worker rose from £31 to £54 a week be-tween 1951 and 1977, with a greater proportionate increase for women (Toland 1979).

Public expenditure doubled during post-war years. There was a significant shift in the tax burden from single people to families from 1969 onwards. Where, between 1961 and 1969, single non-pensioner households paid proportionately more income tax than households with two adults and four children, between 1969 and the mid-1970s, the trend was reversed. Households with two chil-dren and two adults felt the greatest increase in direct taxation, from 9 per cent to 20 per cent.

Spending patterns changed as incomes increased. Most impor-tant was the increase in the number of people buying their own home. In 1951, the majority lived in rented accommodation. By 1978, more than half of all households were owner-occupied and the number of people per dwelling decreased, as young couples and single people found their own homes rather than living with par-ents or relatives. There were other improvements, in the length of education, growth of leisure time, use of 'consumer durables' in the home (taking much of the burden of routine heavy housework off the woman's back) and more common private ownership of cars. The television set was a rarity in the homes of the early fifties. Now it is unusual to find a house without one. Whether an increase in the amount of time spent in front of the box is an improvement in the quality of life, is, of course, debatable, as is the increase in the number of tranquillisers prescribed.

The effects of these and other changes on British social structure have been analysed through surveys conducted by Goldthorpe and Halsey with their colleagues in Oxford (Goldthorpe 1980; Halsey *et al.* 1980). They see British social structure as divided into three main categories. At the top is the class which has expanded enorm-ously in post-war years, the 'service class' consisting of those with professional, administrative and managerial occupations. In the middle is the 'intermediate class' of the routine, non-manual, self-employed, non-professional and lower technical and supervisory occupations. Finally, the 'working class', consisting of the skilled, semi-skilled and unskilled workers. From their 1972 survey of over 10,000 men aged between 20 and 64 years, resident in England and Wales, the most striking feature of the changes they observed was the arrival at the top of many sons of intermediate and working-class fathers (mainly because there was more room at the top).

Although the relative chances of reaching the top remained the same for people of different class-background, the arrival there of greater numbers of socially mobile people is surely of importance in understanding attitudes and behaviour. Although sociologists can demonstrate that equality of opportunity is a myth, most people know from experience that social mobility and improved living standards were possible in these years. The difference in styles of life and widening of opportunities in general, since the war, is one of which all those interviewed were aware. The dominant theme was quite clearly that of upward movement or advancement; this was because they were enjoying, compared to their fathers, greatly improved pay and conditions of employment and in general a much higher standard of living (Goldthorpe 1980). Almost all stressed their improved ability to provide for the well-being of their families. There was a clear awareness of improved security and independence. Of course, with the slowing in the rate of growth of the economy and the reduction in opportunities of recent years, it may well be that the men surveyed by Goldthorpe and Halsey represent a favoured generation. Those who follow them, half a generation or a whole generation behind, are unlikely to experience the same improvement and sense of comparative well-being. Rather, the comparisons they will make with those somewhat older than themselves will encourage feelings of resentment and relative deprivation. The dissatisfaction of the younger disadvantaged generation will disturb the harmony of the post-war years, those feelings of well-being during the 1950s and 1960s which supported the equilibrium of 'consensus politics'.

Over the post-war years, the South-East of England prospered. Migration to the South-East from other regions, and migration from the centres of cities to the outskirts, at the same time, however, produced marked regional and area variations in the quality of living. The increase in the coloured population, a result of the relatively high rates of immigration in the late 1950s and early 1960s, added a further social division. Overlapping geographical, economic and social categories gave a complex picture of inequality, heterogeneity and social incohesion, the effect of which was a significant shift in the framework within which issues were discussed from one of class politics to one of peripheral or marginal groups. The cohesion of the whole was for most of the post-war years held together by a general feeling of contentment. But now the dissatisfaction of the growing numbers in the peripheral groups, especially the young, is being swelled by the increasing resentment of those in the centre, too, who are experiencing a denial of their hopes for the future and a reduction in their feelings of well-being, independence and control. As economic growth has slowed, the material base cannot provide all they have grown accustomed to expect.

Britain is a highly industrialised country. The post-war years saw the growing dominance of the large corporation, employing an increasing proportion of the labour force, and the increasing internationalisation of capital. The 'second industrial revolution', resulting mainly from labour-saving technological change, produced a 'shake out' of manpower in productive industries. Higher incomes were spent on commodities (consumerism) and on services, leading to an increase in employment in both the private and public tertiary sectors. The increase in public sector employment was most marked in local government, rising by 53 per cent between 1961 and 1973, and by 14 per cent in central government in the same period. The proportion of Gross National Product (GNP) passing through the hands of Government consequently grew. At the high point, public expenditure in 1975 accounted for 57 per cent of Gross Domestic Product (GDP) compared with 41 per cent in 1955 and 45 per cent in 1966. Within this, however, about one quarter of national income referred to transfer payments, transfers of income through taxation and social security, from the salaries and wages of the employed to the unemployed and dependent sections of the population, rather than expenditure on goods and services. But the steady rise in public expenditure, particularly in the costs of social expenditure and social security, occurred in the context of a low rate of economic growth. The hope both of Gaitskellites and of progressive Conservatives that an increase in welfare would be financed from the growing wealth of the country proved illusory. In addition, it has been argued that expenditure on welfare is at the expense of the industrial investment required if Britain's long-running economic decline is to be halted. While believing in a compassionate society, some say 'we must get the correct balance between compassion and investment'.

Since 1945 there has been an absolute increase in the population, a reduction in the death-rate and an uneven decline in the birth-rate. The age-structure has altered, increasing the proportion of the dependent population. A steady increase in the divorce rate has occurred at the same time as marriage itself has become more popular (that is, fewer people remain single). The size of families has fallen so that the problem of large families is much reduced compared to pre-war days. But with the predominance of the small 'nuclear family' mode of living, following on social and geographical mobility, suburban living and home-ownership, and a reduction in the use of institutions as a form of care, there has been a rise in the proportion of single-adult households, especially of the old and one-parent families. The vulnerability of these groups to the hazards of life has increased as family and community supports have weakened, especially the help that the old extended family pattern could give to the poorer, needy or solitary members. There has thus occurred not only an increase in the proportion of people who are dependent but also an increase in the range and nature of their dependency.

Rates of unemployment rose, especially in the 1970s. There was also an increase in the 'inactive' population, that is those who were effectively unemployed, having dropped out of the labour force. Peter Jay, for example, calculated the 'effectively unemployed' in 1971 to be 13 per cent of the available labour force. There are great difficulties in measuring these proportions but the trends to an increase in structural unemployment and long-term unemployment are most likely to continue through the 1980s. One of the principal causes of the record post-war levels of unemployment is a profound social change, as more married women now hold jobs or look for them. Between 1974 and 1980, the number of people employed actually held up remarkably well. A fifth of the increase in people out of work was due to a loss of jobs. The remaining four-fifths of those out of work were net new additions to the country's working population. Another way of putting this is to say that the labour market was incapable of expanding to absorb the growing workforce of school-leavers and married women. This problem became serious in the late 1960s. Until then, in the 18 years from 1948, nearly 3 million extra jobs were created in Britain. But between 1966 and 1977 the workforce increased by more than 1 million. The raising of the school-leaving age and Government job creation schemes helped to mask these developments, both policies being adopted in the late sixties and early seventies. The increasing participation of women in the workforce reflected also the shift from manufacturing to service industries. Employment in manufacturing, a male stronghold, has been declining, while employment in service industries grew by nearly 300 per cent after 1948, by 2.1 million jobs. This was especially marked in the public sector, where, between 1971 and 1976, the numbers employed by central Government and local authorities increased by 772,000. More than half of these extra jobs were in health and social services and most of the remainder in education. Public sector employment was to the fore, mainly because it was independent of the declining manufacturing sector (Freud 1978).

At the same time, support weakened for policies which sought to increase taxation on incomes and consumption so as to reduce poverty, improve social security, and expand social services and benefits. As public expenditure rose, the proportion of average income going in taxation also steadily increased, as did the proportion of the population paying tax. Redistribution was predominantly a *horizontal* process, from the occupied to the dependent sections of the population, rather than *vertical*, from rich to poor.

The post-war social legislation removed the most obvious insecurities experienced by the working class as a class. Two decades of full employment and the supplementation of family income by the wages of married women added to this improvement. But the problems of low wage-earners, especially where the wife does not work, of families dependent on a woman's earnings and of 'special groups' outside the labour force have not been solved. The key question for the politics of poverty is that of the relation between these groups and the 'working class'. There has been much debate about the character, composition and degree of 'incorporation' of the working class and of the relation between these changes and political events in post-war years. Undoubtedly, the poor are recruited from the working class. They are its least powerful and most disadvantaged strata. At certain points in their lives, particularly as a child, when bringing up children, or in old age, working-class people are likely to be poor. They run high risks of suffering ill health and disability, unemployment and difficulties with housing, all of which can plunge a family into poverty. But there is also little doubt that subjectively the working class is divided. Many do not recognise shared interests with the poor and disadvantaged. Another rather different question for the politics of welfare is the relation between those employed in the public sector, who, while paying taxes, are aware of their interest in high rates of public expenditure, and those employed in the private (especially manufacturing) sectors, who resent paying taxes to pay for 'the others' – especially as more and more industrial workers, with rising wages and salaries and inflation, come to pay income tax. Political life has reflected and partly encouraged these developments. Group politics – the promotion of sectional interests – and not class politics have characterised the post-war situation.

The inadequacy of British social provision has also come to be recognised as international comparisons have been encouraged through Common Market membership. The European Social Budget 1970–75, produced by the EEC, suggested that Britain's spending on 'social protection' per head of the population was less than half that of Germany, Holland and Denmark and a third lower than that of France. This is the heritage of the failure to finance social expenditure from economic growth. Between 1950 and 1964, a period of increasing affluence, there was no proportionate increase in social service expenditure. Increased wealth was displayed through consumerism, the acquisition of cars, TVs, washing machines and clothing and an increase in home ownership. During the next 15 years, a significant change took place in social policy with an increase in private and occupational welfare schemes, and a growing stress on 'selectivity' rather than 'universality' in the social services.

Demands for increased social expenditure come partly from a desire for improved standards of provision and for a widening of the groups receiving these services and partly from an increase in the proportion of the population requiring them, especially in the number of old, chronically sick, unemployed and one-parent families in our society. The problem has not been solved by the attempt to meet these increasing costs from extra wealth. The solution now involves a choice between three options: one, a redistribution of resources between sections of the population; two, a general reduction in the standard of provision; three, ignoring the needs of specific groups. The persistence of inequality and the problem of relative deprivation reflect the choice not to adopt redistributive policies. The problem of the 'cuts' and cash limits refers to the reduction of standards. And the continuance of absolute poverty demonstrates the rejection of the demands of 'marginal groups'.

A key problem for the social security system has been that national insurance benefits have failed to keep ahead of the supplementary benefit level. The people Beveridge intended to be covered by national insurance have been forced instead to rely on supplementary benefits. Rather than being a last resort, a safety net to catch the few not covered by national insurance, supplementary benefits have become the mainstay of the social security system. In 1948, when national insurance began, nearly three-quarters of the unemployed received unemployment benefit. Now less than half do. One third of all pensioners claim supplementary benefit on top of their retirement pension. Others have received rent and rate rebates to bring their income up to the poverty line. One in ten households in Britain now rely on supplementary benefits for all or part of their income.

In the late seventies, something like 3 million claimants received regular weekly payments of supplementary benefit. One half of these were pensioners and almost a quarter were unemployed. Five million people, that is, claimants and their dependents, relied on supplementary benefits. Many pensioners and families also received financial help from other means-tested benefits, 3,000 of which were administered by local authorities. A major problem with means-tested benefits is low take-up, mainly because the system expects the claimant to take the initiative. Other deterrents are shame and stigma, ignorance and the complexity of leaflets and forms. The institutions dealing with these claims are difficult to locate and hard to penetrate so that only the most persistent and patient get through. A compulsory assessment of entitlement for everyone would be necessary to ensure full take-up of benefits. The growth of the welfare rights movement was an attempt to confront these issues but, in spite of this, take-up of available benefits falls generally short of the total eligible.

Successive Governments have extended the use of means-tested social services. Particularly since 1966, selectivist policies have been adopted under the impact of financial constraints and limits on public expenditure. Increasing use of selective, means-tested benefits produced 'the poverty trap'. This is a 'no-go area' where the systems of taxation and social security overlap. High rates of marginal taxation hit those on the boundary between receiving benefits and not qualifying for them. As Sir Keith Joseph put it 'as soon as a man pops his head above the level of supplementary benefits, he is taxed at 40p in the £'. In this confined space, individual and social problems are exacerbated and political diseases flourish. There are two significant effects: those receiving benefit are kept in the 'poverty trap', creating a 'claiming class'; they are reduced to this dependent situation because of the high costs involved in escaping, since a person in work with low wages may be little better off than if he or she was 'on the benefit'. Additionally, a sense of injustice arises in those just above that level; they feel they are working hard all week, or have worked hard and saved all their lives, to receive little or no higher income than those they think they support from their income tax and national insurance contributions. Their resentment is directed at the people on social security rather than at the system which created the anomaly. The incentives to work and save are diminished in both groups. The contradictory treatment of people on low incomes from work and those on social security, who often live close together, encourages disfavourable attitudes towards the poor, who are seen as 'scroungers'. The main cause of this situation, the poverty trap, is the increasing burden of taxation on the lower paid. Tax thresholds have not been raised sufficiently to offset the effects of inflation, thus creating the phenomenon of 'fiscal drag', wherein more and more people are hauled into the tax net, especially strange at a time when higher rates of taxation are cut, as after the General Election of 1979.

The centrality of the insurance principle in social security provision, combined with an increasing use of selective benefits for those 'in greatest need', has thus created a deep divide between people at work and people not at work. Another significant feature of the post-war situation has been the growth of occupational welfare schemes, especially occupational pensions and sickness schemes, together with the adoption of the earnings-related rather than flat-rate principle for certain contributions and benefits. These have maintained and exacerbated inequality. Rather than redressing imbalance, welfare provision now reflects wage and salary differentials. Occupational welfare schemes and fringe benefits have increasingly been offered as inducements to retain the allegiance of staff and workers hired and trained at a rising cost, thus further increasing the differences among employees. Those receiving considerable benefits are divided from those who do not. This is mainly a division between non-manual and manual workers and sectional bargaining between trade unions and management for improved benefits has consequently stifled demands for improvement in the statutory field. This has all helped to strengthen the belief that the State scheme is residual, providing only for those who cannot help themselves, at a lower standard. A hierarchy of welfare provision has been created: at the top, private and occupational welfare, supported by the 'hidden welfare' of tax allowances on, especially, pensions, life insurance and housing, these being of more advantage to those paying tax and to the higher paid. Below these, the earnings-related national insurance schemes, especially pensions, although unemployment and sickness benefits were earnings-related until the early 1980s. At the bottom, supplementary benefits for those left out of the other schemes. Supplementary benefits are not, however, a residual provision for a declining minority but a permanent one for a substantial and increasing population group.

The low rates of benefit provided through the national insurance system have been a persistent problem. Instigated mainly by cost-cutting considerations, the level of supplementary benefits has been raised more frequently than that of national insurance benefits in an attempt to direct resources to those in greatest need. Although, in general, national insurance benefits have not reached a subsistence level (using a poverty line defined by reference to the consistently rising level of supplementary benefits) insurance benefits have been increased several times since 1948. At present they are higher than when first introduced, even after taking into account the rise in prices. In real terms, the overall level of benefits in the thirty years from 1948 just kept pace with average earnings, benefits for a married couple usually amounting to about 30 per cent of the average wage (Young 1974: 7). Debate on the indexing of benefits, that is whether to link them with prices or average earnings, refers to the desire, or not, to maintain the value of benefits or link them to any rise in national prosperity. The paying of earnings-related benefits, mainly in the late sixties and seventies, had most to do with the rise in the overall level of benefits received. This overall level must be distinguished clearly from the flat-rate level of benefit, and from the level of supplementary benefit, these being more relevant to the problem of poverty. The aim of the partially abolished earnings-related benefits was to increase security by maintaining a standard of living through brief periods of sickness or unemployment or in the few years of retirement.

Want and poverty have been increasingly attacked through the provision of selective benefits. The main groups in poverty are old people, the unemployed, low wage-earners, the chronically sick and disabled and single-parent families. Social policies have been directed separately at these social categories, with varying effect. The problem of poverty in old age has been pre-eminent. Discussion of pensions schemes dominated from the late fifties to the late seventies, with various proposals being put forward by the parties and alternating Governments modifying and replacing the proposals of their predecessors. A rational pensions scheme was finally introduced in 1978, having been delayed for several years as the issue was used as a political football by the two parties in the stylised electoral competitions of those years.

The Social Security Pensions Act 1975 was based on the Labour

Government's White Paper of 1974, *Better Pensions*, though its proposals went back to 1969 when the White Paper, *Superannuation and Social Insurance*, was published. The proposed legislation was then interrupted by a change of government, when the Conservative Government published its alternative proposals, *Strategy for Pensions*. Another change in government in 1974 prevented the consequent legislation, the 1973 Social Security Act, coming into operation. The debate over pensions was a key one between Labour and Conservatives, partly because of the size of the constituency of old-age pensioners, about 8 million voters, and partly because of the significance of pensions within the total social security budget and its effect on public expenditure levels. The main issue dividing the parties was the extent to which state or private enterprise should be responsible for the earnings-related portion additional to the basic pension. The new arrangements which came into effect in April 1978 divided the pension into two parts: the basic flat rate plus a certain percentage, about 25 per cent of earnings. Contributions would be earnings-related and tripartite, from employers, employees and Government. The basic pension would be paid by the State while the additonal pension would be paid either by the State *or* by employers where they operated an acceptable occupational scheme and contracted out. The scheme would mature over 20 years and anyone retiring within 20 years would receive a proportion of the full entitlement. Benefits included not only retirement pensions, but also invalidity pensions, widows' (but not necessarily widowers') pensions and widowed mothers' allowances. The rate of benefit would be revalued to keep pace with either earnings or prices (exactly which in practice being an issue between Labour and Conservatives). Pension rights would be safeguarded during absences from employment and on changes of employment. The aim was to remove the dependence of old people on supplementary benefits when retired.

To tackle the problem of poverty caused by low pay, the Conservatives introduced the Family Income Supplement (FIS) in their Social Security Act 1971. This aimed to help the low-paid with children. Where gross family income fell below an officially prescribed level (£67 from November 1980 for a one-child family), a supplement would be paid equal to half of this deficiency, up to a maximum of £17 per week. The prescribed level would vary with the number of children. The Family Income Supplement aimed to benefit most those single parents and families on low incomes who might, when out of work, fall subject to the 'wage-stop' (in existence until 1975), since FIS would be regarded as part of their previous normal income.

A further attempt to improve the situation of poorer families was the child benefit scheme of 1978, introduced by Labour, although discussions had been initiated by the Conservatives as they attempted to formulate a practicable negative income tax scheme. The aim was to raise the erstwhile family allowance to a level high enough to have some real effect on the circumstances of families and also to increase the differential between the working and the non-working poor. The Child Benefit Act aimed to implement an important Beveridge proposal, that for adequate family allowances. Adequate child benefits would help children in poverty – a quarter of the very poor are children – single-parent families and the low-paid, some of the major categories in poverty. The provisions of the Act would phase out family allowances and the income tax allowances for dependent children and replace both with a new child benefit. This non-contributory benefit would be payable for all children, including the first. It represented part of the Government's response to the 1974 Finer Committee's Report, *One-Parent Families*, and the evidence collected in surveys of the poor and publicised by Child Poverty Action Group in particular. These benefits have not, however, kept pace with the cost of living and have been allowed to fall behind again. If paid at an adequate level, they would effectively reduce the amount of poverty through a universal benefit, based on a redistribution of income from the better-off to the less well-off and from those without dependent children to families. They would also redistribute income from men to women, in that tax allowances generally benefited men, whereas child benefits are usually collected by women.

Thus attempts have been made to introduce measures which would help special groups known to be most likely to be in poverty. With varying effectiveness and enthusiasm, changes have been made aimed at helping the old and children, especially of the low-paid and single parents. Those most noticeably ignored and neglected have been the unemployed and, to a lesser extent, the sick and disabled.

Other ways of tackling the problem have concentrated on administrative reforms. The evidence of the 1950s and 1960s demonstrated that large numbers of persons eligible for benefit, especially old people, did not claim. In the early 1960s, nearly 1 million retirement pensioners entitled to national assistance were not receiving it. In an attempt to improve take-up and eliminate stigma, the 1966 Social Security Act was introduced, establishing in legislation for the first time in Britain the term 'social security'. The national insurance and national assistance schemes were to be linked more closely. As part of the same mood, national assistance was renamed supplementary benefits. A concern with administrative reorganisation dominated, with the Ministry of Social Security assuming overall responsibility and replacing the Ministry of Pensions and National Insurance.

The most important aspect of these otherwise superficial changes was the replacement of the National Assistance Board by the Supplementary Benefits Commission (SBC), a semi-autonomous body acting as a sub-department of the Ministry of Social Security. In 1968, the Department of Health and Social Security was created by amalgamating the Ministry of Social Security with the Ministry of Health. Internally, sections dealt with social security, health and personal social services, and each had an Advisory Committee of members from public authorities, trade unions and the professions. The aim of the reorganisation was to coordinate benefits in kind with benefits in cash. Whether effective coordination was achieved, however, is open to doubt. The merger reflected the mood of the times: the attempt was to develop a strong State, to involve State institutions in active intervention in the economy, to promote industrial reorganisation and changes in the attendant social arrangements. In retrospect, the institutional changes associated with these strategies appear more symbolic than effective. The only important change politically was the establishment of the SBC, and to a lesser extent the Advisory Committees, as 'governing institutions', providing a pathway of influence for specific groups separate from the traditional route through party and Parliament. How substantial were the changes and how far superficial window-dressing?

Entitlement to benefit under specified conditions was emphasised. Some of the reluctance to claim due to stigma, ignorance and bureaucratic complexity may have been reduced, but Beveridge's proposals to provide benefit as long as the need remained and at subsistence level were still not accepted. The division between insurance and assistance remained. The administration of social security continued to contain a punitive and controlling element. The introduction of the four-week rule in 1968, to try to control the 'work-shy', and the continuance of the wage-stop until 1975 are cases in point, aiming to discipline labour and maintain the incentive to work.

From the sixties onwards, the direction of social policy changed to the use of more selective benefits. The Labour Party had since 1931 viewed means tests with abhorrence but in spite of this, selectivism increased. The Conservative Party in the early seventies introduced a number of new selective benefits. In the discussion of universalism versus selectivism, it is worth noting that the most redistributive social benefits are those which are most highly selective. Although, until recently, the take-up rate for FIS and housing allowances was less than 50 per cent, FIS is still the most redistributive of social security benefits. Sixty-nine per cent of this expenditure went to the bottom 20 per cent (of the income distribution) in 1976. Supplementary benefits were also concentrated where most needed, 63 per cent going to the lowest 20 per cent. Of unemployment benefit, by contrast, only 42 per cent went to this bottom group, the rest being fairly evenly spread. Long-term and short-term national insurance benefits, sickness and industrial injury benefits were spread among the middle groups. So the most beneficial of benefits for low income households are supplementary benefits, rent and rate rebates and old-age pensions. The least specifically beneficial for them are short-term national insurance benefits, sickness and industrial injury benefits and child benefits. This difference reflects the differing purposes of social security, one being the relief of poverty, the other the reduction of insecurity which is itself, of course, as Beveridge argued, a measure helping to prevent poverty. The argument that resources should be concentrated on the poor ignores the obvious fact that the numbers of the poor would increase were the incomes of middle groups reduced. If there were no taxes or transfers, 30 per cent of households in 1976 would have been below the level of income defining the bottom 20 per cent. If transfers alone were taken into account, 16 per cent only would have been in the bottom group. (The effect of tax payments at that time increased the relative poverty of households with children, so that, because of tax payment, a further 4 per cent were recruited to the bottom group – a clear effect of the hardship caused to low income households by the lowering of tax thresholds in recent years (DHSS April 1978).) The poverty trap is a very complex phenomenon, caused by the interrelation of national insurance payments, rent and rate rebates, FIS, payments of income tax, national insurance graduated payments, the erstwhile free school meals and welfare milk, all exacerbated by housing costs and work expenses.

The lack of integration and coordination in the total social welfare system, fiscal, occupational and State, reflects the ambiguity and lack of clear definition that exists regarding the purposes of social security. But in spite of its deficiencies, the system is redistributive – the greatest proportional benefit goes to households of one, two or three adults without any children in the lowest income ranges, mainly retired people living on supplementary benefits and the chronically sick and disabled. There is a considerable redistribution overall from larger incomes to smaller ones and from smaller families to larger ones. Those whose need is greatest receive from those in less need – a gain for the lowest income groups, large families and the old; offset, however, by gains to those who make most use of the health and education systems, who seem more likely to be middle class. Redistribution is mainly from the working population, irrespective of income, to those who cannot earn and from small families to larger ones. Social services in general are provided at the expense of the great bulk of moderate earners with few dependents. Compared with European countries, social assistance through a test of need and means plays a larger part in Britain.

Supplementary benefits are provided as of right on a non-contributory basis. Supplementary allowance is paid to those fit for work who are not in full-time work. They are required to register for work (sign on), before receiving it. Payment is calculated on the difference between a person's income and his requirements as laid down on a scale, plus rent and any additions for which he might be eligible. Supplementary pension is payable to those over retirement age and not in full-time work, calculated on the same basis as supplementary allowance, although the basic scale is higher. A certain amount of income is disregarded in calculating the total supplement due, for example, a certain amount of weekly earnings and income from other sources, as well as capital up to a specified level. Not all rent is paid, for example, if it is considered excessive. Family Income Supplement is payable weekly but calculated for twelve months at a time. Supplementary benefits have usually entitled the recipient to free prescriptions, dental treatment and other NHS supplies and some other means-tested services, when and where available, such as free school meals, free further education and some free milk and transport.

The major problem facing the social security system in the early 1980s is the rise in the number of people under pension age dependent on supplementary benefit. The main factor contributing to this has been the rising rate of unemployment which shows little sign of abating in the near future, reflecting the fact that most of those presently employed show little real concern with this issue. The risks of unemployment are not evenly shared. If unemployment were spread equally, each person would be unemployed once every six years. In fact, in any one year, only 3 per cent of the labour force account for 70 per cent of the weeks of unemployment (Metcalf 1979). The social security system does not meet the needs of this group, since only two-fifths of the unemployed are covered by the national insurance system – the rest have to apply for means-tested supplementary benefit. These long-term unemployed and their families are the poorest of the poor. So much for the belief that unemployment in the 1980s, unlike that in the 1930s, is 'cushioned'. Dependence on supplementary benefits does not only cause hardship to the recipients – hardship which is well documented. The system itself is in danger of breaking down. The clerks at the desks bear the brunt of this but to their frustration should be added the increasing cost of administration. The administrative cost of supplementary benefits in the late 1970s was over three times that of national insurance. This was the result of each case being considered individually, with various rates of benefit being awarded to different needs and the overall income and resources of each claimant being assessed before benefit could be awarded. It was these pressures which led to the 1978 Review, *Social Assistance* which culminated in the 1980 Social Security Act. The significant features of this review of the administrative arrangements affecting the payment of supplementary benefit were that it was conducted by a team appointed internally within the DHSS and that it accepted from the outset a nil-cost assumption. It also presumed there would be no changes in other government departments. Consequently the scope for a radical attack on the problems of the social security system was severely curtailed. The changes proposed, most of which were incorporated into the 1980 Social Security Act, were to adapt the system to 'its mass role of coping with millions of claimants in known and readily defined categories'. The main aim was to standardise provision instead of treating individuals as discrete cases. The principle of discretionary payments was indeed one which led to the greatest pressure on the clerks in the local offices, to complaints of discrimination and to anomalies. In 1976, 49 per cent of all claimants received Exceptional Circumstances Additions (ECAs). The majority (78%) were supplementary pensioners. About 66 per cent of supplementary pensioners received ECAs, compared with 34 per cent of the sick and disabled, 30 per cent of lone parents and only 19 per cent of the unemployed. The special expenses most commonly involved were for extra heating (63% of the total), diet (19%) and laundry (8%). Exceptional Needs Payments (ENPs) were received by 26 per cent of claimants and 7 per cent had been refused one. Exceptional Needs Payments went more to claimants under pension age, those most likely to receive them being lone parents. Over half the ENPs (52%) were for clothing, 13 per cent for bedding, 18 per cent for furniture or household equipment and 6 per cent for fuel (DHSS July 1978).

David Donnison, the Chairman of the SBC until 1980, pointed out cryptically that if all 3 million claimants (and another million who may be entitled to claim but are not yet doing so) were to ask for everything they might get, the service would simply collapse. To protect itself from the real danger of chaos (already threatening a few local offices) the service has to rely on 'rationing' procedures of some kind – on things like claimants' ignorance of their rights and on delays, lost files and the generally forbidding character of the system.

The administrative reforms suggested by the DHSS team, and incorporated into the 1980 Social Security Act, aim to restore control of the machine and defuse the flash-points by reducing the amount of contact between officers and claimants. The effect is, of course, also to cut down the extent to which individual needs are met and to increase the arbitrariness of the system.

The Social Security Act of 1980 provided the occasion to absorb the SBC within the DHSS, thus further reducing the extent to which the interests of the poor could be represented to Government.

In the 1980 budget it was announced that earnings-related supplements would be abolished. At the same time the Conservative Chancellor proposed the de-indexing of short-term unemployment and sickness benefits but the linking of old-age pensions and long-term supplementary benefits to price rises. These changes added a further complication to an already over-burdened system and increased the potential for anomalies. The conflicting interests of Governments in protecting the 'very weak' while at the same time disciplining labour and cutting public expenditure have produced the confused and contradictory system that remains with us in spite of the reforms of 1980.

Two-thirds of the total financial cost of social insurance goes on retirement pensions. The great bulk of social assistance payment

have been made in supplementation of insurance benefits, especially old-age pensions but also to widows and the chronically sick.
Total expenditure on social security has risen faster than the
National Product mainly due to the growing proportion of old people in the population. The goals of the system thought to have been
established in the 1940s were to provide an adequate minimum
income in time of need (cash benefits), and to enable equal opportunity of access to services (benefits in kind). But the continuance
of poverty has been repeatedly demonstrated in the past thirty
years. Why has the social security system failed? Mainly this has to
do with the low rates of benefit provided through national insurance and the failure to apply for the benefits to which they are
entitled of large numbers, particularly the old. Poverty among low
wage-earners, partially alleviated by FIS, has been exacerbated by
the lowering of tax thresholds and the inadequacy of child benefit
rates.

Three systems of welfare coexist in Britain in the 1980s: (1) private welfare, occupational and insurance schemes; (2) State and
social security provisions; and (3) fiscal welfare (Titmuss 1958: 34).
Total welfare, the distribution of incomes and the extent of poverty
are affected not only by gross earnings but also by levels of tax and
national insurance contributions, the ownership of assets, fringe
benefits, gifts from relatives, consumption of public social services
and differential access to them, and tax allowances. The system at
present is one which lacks coordination: it consists of 'fragmented,
piecemeal measures bristling with anomalies' (Townsend 1976:
285), the very situation Beveridge had aimed to overcome. Underlying the whole system is a lack of finance which has led to a retreat
from universalistic to selectivist measures and continuing low levels
of benefit. The Supplementary Benefits Commission itself in its
evidence to the Royal Commission on the Distribution of Income
and Wealth described benefits for the poor as 'barely adequate to
meet their needs at a level that is consistent with full participation
in the relatively wealthy society in which they live'. Administrative
problems remain: dingy offices, long queues, harassed and low-
paid clerical officers; erratic treatment of different claimants; low
rate of take-up due to ignorance, lack of organisation, administrative evasiveness, malpractice, inefficiency and pride. The needs of
significant groups are not adequately met, especially those of one-
parent families and the long-term unemployed.

Asked the question 'why does poverty remain in relatively
affluent Britain', some would reply that the explanation lies obvi-

ously with the inefficiencies and inadequacies of our social security system. It seems clear so far that this must be part of the answer, but others would prefer to lay the blame on the poor themselves. In the next chapter we shall consider how far the problem can be clarified by knowledge of the numbers and characteristics of the poor.

Chapter three

WHO ARE THE POOR?

The poor are not only people living on supplementary benefit but also those whose pay from work is not enough to provide a decent standard of living. These are people who are at a disadvantage in the competition for work or limited in their choice of job – perhaps because they have family responsibilities, like the care of children or other relatives. Or they may be unhealthy, physically or mentally handicapped or old. They may be discriminated against on the grounds of race, sex or age; or they may live in areas where there are few job opportunities. Poor people are mainly the underskilled and underqualified. They see themselves 'as rough people, humble people, unsuited for positions that hold responsibility. The positions they hold are at the receiving end; they take the jobs that are available, benefits they are given, the accommodation they are allocated. They accept and make do.' (Wilson and Herbert 1978: vii) In the complexity of bureaucratic society they have little power to make demands, either individually or collectively. They lose out continually, suffer frustrations, take knocks and blows which damage self-esteem and dignity and further reduce their freedom of choice.

THE PROBLEM OF MEASUREMENT

The main questions asked in most studies of poverty have been – how many people are poor? And what are the causes of poverty? Almost all studies of poverty are based on one of two types of data: those which use official statistics usually derive from data collected for other purposes, especially those conducted to help construct economic indicators, like the Retail Price Index. The other main type of study is that of the independent survey carried out by professionals.

When assessing the conclusions of the various studies of poverty, it is important to look carefully at the methods and techniques of measurement used. The two key questions to ask are – how is the income defined? Is it in terms of the individual, the family or the household? And how are the budgets of different sizes of such income units compared? For example, when family income is compared, some adjustment must be made to allow for the different needs and commitments of different kinds of families. Account has to be taken of customary expenditure patterns, whether or not expenditure is efficient, and whether or not there are other resources, such as undeclared income, gifts, or the use of public services to which a cash value can be applied. Some of these adjustments are easier than others to make and studies vary in the way they take these factors into account.

Results are also affected by the source of data used. In Britain, studies are usually based on official government statistics and surveys. Official statistics tend to be comprehensive and, as regards public debate, have the virtue of appearing to be neutral. At least, it is unlikely that government reports would deliberately over-estimate the incidence of poverty. Collected regularly and over time, these studies allow comparisons to be made, attracting as they do higher response rates than independent studies. However, since many of the poor are not at work and are dependent on social security, income tax returns are of little use in studies of poverty and the main sources of data are the *Household Expenditure Survey* of 1953–54 and the *Family Expenditure Surveys* which have been undertaken continuously since 1957. The latter in particular provide a body of data stretching back over 20 years. The major drawbacks are that the surveys exclude individuals living in institutions and also assume some sharing of resources within households and families. They tend therefore to underestimate the extent of poverty experienced by individuals.

The supplementary benefit scale-rates are generally taken as the poverty line in studies based on official statistics. One problem with this is that these scales have themselves changed over time. In 'real' terms, the benefit scales have risen substantially in post-war years, as indicated by the work of Fiegehen, Lansley and Smith (1977), which shows that by 1971 standards the proportion *in* poverty in 1973 (that is, living *below* the level which would be provided by supplementary benefit) was less than one-fortieth of the population (2.3 per cent of individuals, 1.3 million people). Using the same 1971 standard, over one-fifth would have been regarded as poor in

1953–54 (that is, 21 per cent of individuals or 10.6 million people). However, using the lower national assistance standard, which applied in 1953–54, only 5 per cent of the population would be defined as poor in that year and only 0.2 per cent in 1973. It has, however, been argued that a rise in real income does not denote an equivalent rise in the real standard of living, since the price of necessities may have risen faster than average prices, as measured by the Retail Price Index, and new 'necessities' may have emerged. Nevertheless, these features cannot account for all of the rise in supplementary benefit rates. The change in their real value over time reflects the general increase in prosperity in Britain in these years. The difference made to the proportions found in poverty by the use of different years' supplementary benefit scales is demonstrated again in the same study (Fiegehen *et al.* 1977). This shows that when the supplementary benefit scales of 1973 are applied to the 1973 data (surely the most appropriate procedure), the numbers living below the poverty line become 7.1 per cent of households or 4.9 per cent of individuals, a total of 2.6 million people.

If one were to refer to total expenditure rather than to total income, rather more households would be designated as poor: 9.4 per cent compared to 7.1 per cent.

Another variation in findings has to do with the difference between the categorisations 'households' and 'tax units'. Where the tax unit rather than the household is considered, the proportion of poor individuals rises from 4.9 per cent to 8.8 per cent. This mainly reflects the situation of single people sharing households (70 per cent of all poor tax units are single people). These would be largely old people living with relatives. Thus, as Fiegehen says, 'without proper formulation or due qualification, no unambiguous answer can be given to the question, how many people are in poverty at a given time' (Fiegehen *et al.* 1977: 47).

COUNTING THE POOR

Most of the studies which describe and count the poor focus on income, principally because such information is available for the population as a whole and over time and is amenable to standardisation and quantitative analysis.

One conclusion which emerges clearly from these studies is that throughout the twentieth century there has been a substantial rise in the importance of old age in causing poverty. This is the result of demographic change and of the trend to earlier retirement. Since

Rowntree's first study at the end of the last century, there has been a decline in the importance of large families in contributing to the total numbers in poverty. However, large families still run a high risk of being poor and the total number of children living in poverty is also very large. A further conclusion of these studies is that the number of people who during their life-time experience poverty is much higher than the proportion found to be poor at any one time.

The first major survey in the post-war years to show that poverty continued to be a problem was published by Brian Abel-Smith and Peter Townsend as *The Poor and The Poorest* in 1965. This study is the basis for comparative work on the situation in Britain in the post-war years. They compared the incidence of poverty in 1953–54 with that in 1960, using data from government income and expenditure surveys. Their primary aim was to consider what changes had occurred during the 1950s. They defined the poor as those having a low level of living, that is, having an income below 140 per cent of the basic National Assistance Scale and they concluded that there had been an increase in the numbers and the proportion of the population living in poverty between 1953 and 1960. There had been, in particular, a marked increase in the proportion living below the poverty line. The poor had been 10.1 per cent of households and 7.8 per cent of persons in 1953–54. In 1960, these figures had risen to 17.9 per cent of households and 14.2 per cent of persons. The number of the poorest, that is those living below the poverty line, had been 2.1 per cent of households and 1.2 per cent of persons in 1953–54. They had risen to 4.7 per cent of households and 3.8 per cent of persons by 1960. The reasons for this increase, they concluded, were the increase in the number of the aged and an increase in the proportion of large families in the population since 1953. The number of families with dependent children had increased by 20 per cent but the number of families with six or more children had increased by 45 per cent. Another factor had been the increase in the number of the chronically sick, particularly of men in the age group 55–65 years.

Abel-Smith and Townsend thus demonstrated that, contrary to popular opinion, the numbers in poverty had been growing throughout the 1950s. Until they published these results, only one major piece of research had been carried out in the post-war years. This was Rowntree and Lavers' study of York which showed that only 1.5 per cent of its survey population lived in poverty in 1950, compared with 18 per cent in 1936 (Rowntree and Lavers 1951). A leader in *The Times* had commented that this was a 'remarkable improvement – no less than the virtual abolition of the sheerest want'. Rowntree and Lavers had concluded that full employment and rising wage-rates were mainly responsible for this improvement. In 1936, 60 per cent of poverty had been due to unemployment or low wages; this was reduced to only 1 per cent in 1950. Peter Townsend, however, doubted these conclusions. He challenged the validity of Rowntree's minutely calculated subsistence scales, mainly on the basis that the list of 'necessary expenditures' was too narrow. In 1958, he pointed out that about 2.25 million people were dependent at any one time on national assistance allowances, most of them for extremely long periods. He emphasised that when talking of poverty one was referring to the 'submerged fifth' of the population, nearer 10 million than 5 million people (Townsend 1958).

It is remarkable that so little research on poverty was conducted in the 1940s and 1950s. Income-poverty was not considered to be a problem. Poor housing was seen as the remaining social problem and the hope for its solution to lie in slum-clearance programmes. Disproportionate attention was given to the problems of 'affluence'.

With the 'rediscovery of poverty', promoted by writers like Abel-Smith and Townsend in Great Britain and Michael Harrington in the USA, more studies of poverty have been undertaken. One commentator has referred to this as *The Poverty Business* and has argued that this effort produced more benefit to social scientists and social workers than to the poor themselves (Higgins 1978). But with all this evidence we ought to be less ignorant now about the size of the problem and the characteristics of the poor. However, there is confusion about what the 'facts' are and even more disagreement about how they should be interpreted and acted upon.

The evidence of the late 1950s and early 1960s indicated that there were large numbers of older people, widows and even the families of people in full-time employment who were still living below the national assistance standard. The trend seemed to be that poverty far from disappearing was actually increasing. How does the evidence appear from the stand-point of the 1970s? The National Institute of Economic and Social Research (NIESR) report emphasises that the 'real incomes' of the poorer groups in society have increased by about 50–55 per cent, since 1953 (Fiegehen *et al.* 1977). However, in spite of this absolute rise in living standards, the relative standard of the poor has remained approximately constant (at about 49 per cent of the median for the fifth percentile and at about 58 per cent for the tenth percentile) That is to say, the standard of living of the poorer groups in Britain is about half of that of the 'man in the middle' and this has been the case throughout the post-war years. Increased prosperity, resulting mainly from full employment and economic growth, has raised living standards all round but this has not affected the distribution of incomes. There has been no redistribution in favour of the poorer groups. The NIESR survey concludes, 'the evidence points to neither a significant deterioration nor an improvement in the relative incomes of the poor over this period' (op. cit. : p. 29).

THE CHARACTERISTICS OF THE POOR

Households dependent on someone under the age of 20 years or on someone over 55 years run a higher risk of poverty. In other age-groups, factors other than age are more powerful in explaining poverty, such as unemployment, sickness and broken families. The most important systematic cause of poverty in later years is certainly retirement. Where a woman is the head of the house, the risk of poverty is greater. Eighteen per cent of households headed by a woman are in poverty compared to 4 per cent where the head is a man.

When households are analysed, the characteristics associated with poverty are:
where one person lives alone;
where there are one or two retired people; where the head of the house is at least 65 years old or is retired; where the head of the house is a woman;
where the head of the house is not at work;
where the main source of income is social security benefit; and
where the household has only one source of income.

A quarter of all those living in poverty are children. The stress which has generally been laid on the contribution of old age to the problem of poverty has tended to blind us to the fact that over half of all individuals in poverty are either children or adults of working age. In 1971, the population in poverty (i.e. living below the poverty line) totalled 2,613,000: 628,000 were children (24%); 787,000 were of working age (30.1%); and 1,198,000 were retired (45.9%) (Fiegehen *et al.* 1977). The families of the unemployed are increasingly likely to be living in poverty. Even in 1971, 20 per cent of households where the head was unemployed were living below the poverty line.

Households which are dependent on social security as their principal source of income are likely to be living in poverty: perhaps surprisingly, 29 per cent of such households had incomes below the supplementary benefit level. Sixty-seven per cent of poor individuals are entirely dependent on social security. Where the head of the household is not at work, either because this is a single-parent family, where employment is difficult to combine with the responsibility for children, or where he or she is chronically sick or no longer seeking work, 19 per cent of such households would be found to be living in poverty.

The poverty of 73 per cent of all poor individuals can be attributed to immediate 'social' factors, such as old age or being in a single-parent family. Twenty-seven per cent of poor individuals' poverty can be said to be caused directly by 'economic' factors such as low wages or unemployment. Of course, underlying the 'social' factors are contingencies of the labour market which affect job opportunities and conditions of work and determine required capacities. For example, the poverty of many old-age pensioners results from a history of periodic unemployment during their working lives and employment in low-paid work from which they are unlikely to have received an occupational pension or been able to accumulate many savings.

Table 1. Demographic and economic causes of poverty (percentages)

	Causes	
Characteristics of head of household	*Mainly demographic*	*Mainly economic*
Employment hindered by:		
Retirement and /or old age	48	
Being a single parent	10	
Being female (not retired)	5	
Other reasons (unoccupied)	7	
Available for employment but:		
Unemployed		10
Employed, 4–6 children	3	
Low income from:		
Self-employment		10
Employment		7
All poor individuals	73	27

Source: (Fiegehen 1977: 66, Table 5.8)

The poor are more likely to be drawn from those living in privately rented accommodation or council housing than from owner-occupiers. Forty-five per cent of those in poverty lived in council housing (31 per cent of all households lived in council housing), and 28 per cent in privately rented accommodation (19 per cent of all households were in privately rented accommodation) compared to 26 per cent who were owner-occupiers (47 per cent of all households lived in owner-occupied housing in 1971).

The data referred to above, which derive from the NIESR study, use measures which depict poverty in its lowest terms. They refer to poverty as the condition of those living *below* the level which would be provided by supplementary benefit, and they refer to *households* rather than *families*, thus assuming some sharing of income within households, between families or cohabitants. The figures referred to above on the numbers and characteristics of the poor are of those indisputably living in poverty and living in the most severe conditions defined by income alone. Other sources of poverty, for example housing and environmental conditions, are excluded. The number of those in poverty, still using this official definition of poverty, would rise to 4.75 million were the nuclear family rather than the household to be considered. The numbers would rise also were one to include those living on the poverty line, that is receiving the minimum as laid down by Parliament in supplementary benefit scale rates and no more. Frank Field and Peter Townsend, writing in 1975, focused attention on the number of people with incomes up to 110 per cent of the supplementary benefit level and concluded that poverty had almost doubled between 1960 and 1972 (Field and Townsend 1975).

The 'comeback of poverty' has been discussed by Frank Field who sees every indication that the numbers in poverty will continue to grow (Field 1978). In 1978 there were 1.5 million unemployed: by August 1980 the critical figure of 2 million had been reached. Forecasts indicate that by 1982 at least 3 million will be unemployed. Between 1947 and 1977, the proportion of the unemployed who depended exclusively on supplementary benefit rose from 10 per cent to 42 per cent, mainly due to an increase in long-term unemployment. The total number of people dependent on supplementary benefit at the time of writing this is 5 million.

LOW INCOMES

If one looks at information on low-income households, that is the bottom 20 per cent, using data from the 1975 Family Expenditure Survey, a similar picture to that described above emerges (Van Slooten and Coverdale 1977). The equivalent incomes of these households, in December 1975, were less than or equal to £32.27 per week. This compares with the long-term supplementary benefit scale rate (including an allowance for housing costs) at that time for a married couple of £26.50. Thus the bottom 20 per cent was composed of households with incomes at or below the supplementary benefits scale rate plus 20 per cent. These low-income households contained 17 per cent of all individuals but 38 per cent of pensioners. The variation in living standards in British society is shown by the fact that the bottom 20 per cent of households received only 10 per cent of equivalent net income. The share of the top 20 per cent of households at that time was 35 per cent. As we have seen, the majority of low-income households are pensioner households. A second common group are households with children, since the characteristics of those on low incomes mirror those defined as 'in poverty'. However, the gross income of only 17 per cent of the two-parent low-income households in this survey came from social security benefits – pointing quite clearly to the contribution of low wages to the problem. It is interesting to note in this connection that low-income households with children paid 16 per cent of their gross income in direct taxes (income tax plus national insurance), not a great deal less than the 21 per cent paid on average by other households with children. Low-income households spent a third of their income on food; other households spent only a quarter of their income on food. They also spent more on housing and on fuel and light, to a large extent reflecting the additional time spent at home by pensioners and children.

The supplementary benefit level plays a prominent part in studies of poverty. It is worth noting, therefore, that in post-war years the average Briton has lived only at between two and three times the supplementary benefit level. Since 'average earnings' figure so largely in popular discussions, it should also be remembered that 'the man in the middle' earns only 91 per cent of the average; that is, more than half of all workers earn less than the average. Almost two-thirds of families have a net income worth less than twice what they would receive as long-term supplementary benefit; and three-quarters of families have incomes worth less than two and a half times the value of their long-term supplementary benefit rate.

Most of the poorest receive their incomes from the State: pensioners, the unemployed, the sick and the disabled and one-parent families. One major characteristic of the poor is that, in general, they are excluded from the labour market. This outsider and dependent status is a critical feature of their situation. However, as should be clear by now, some low wage-earners also live in poverty. These are people on the edges of the labour force. However, a straight correlation between low pay and poverty is difficult to make since most of the low-paid are women. Where the woman is the head of the household, as we have seen, the risk of poverty is greater. But most women's earnings are additional to the earnings of the husband and act to lift a household out of poverty, although in themselves the wages of either the man or the woman (but especially of the woman) would be insufficient to support the family. The crucial role of joint earnings, that is, of the necessity for both adults to earn an income, is shown by the fact that where the wife does not work and where there are several children, one finds the poorest working families. Although, as discussed above, large families do not contribute to poverty in the way they did before the war, 8 per cent of children are living in poverty (at or below the supplementary benefit level) and, what is more alarming, a quarter of all Britain's children are *poor* (that is, they live in families with incomes below 140 per cent of the supplementary benefit level).

POVERTY AND DEPRIVATION

The conclusion of Peter Townsend's impressive survey of *Poverty in the United Kingdom* is that almost a third of the British population is poor (Townsend 1979). He found that 9 per cent were living below the poverty line and a further 23 per cent on the margins of poverty – findings that broadly confirm existing estimates of the incidence of poverty. The larger class of those on the margins of poverty forms the reservoir from which the very poor are drawn. From Townsend's findings we can conclude that since a third of the people are poor, a solution to the problem of poverty can only lie in transferring resources from the top third to the middle and lower thirds, through an equitable and acceptable incomes policy and a wealth tax. The incomes of the middle class and elite would have to be reduced for an attack on poverty to be effective. There is just not enough 'fat' in the bottom half of incomes to provide the resources for a solution. Townsend also demonstrates that the risks of poverty are not evenly shared, that there is a life-cycle of poverty and that the division between manual and non-manual workers continues to be a crucial one.

One of his more striking findings is that the imputed income from social service benefits of the richest 20 per cent is nearly four times that of the bottom 20 per cent, deriving mainly from the value of education and mortgage tax relief. Townsend emphasises that poverty is an integral part of an elaborate hierarchy of wealth and esteem. In fact, Townsend's book, although called *Poverty in the United Kingdom*, can be seen as a classic study of British social structure, for it tells us as much about the rich as about the poor.

Two different concepts of the causes of poverty are common. Those which try to explain how poverty is created in society conclude, as Townsend does, that the social structure is the root cause, especially as it produces an inequitable distribution of rewards. Studies which limit themselves to the presentation of data, on the other hand, narrow the definition of 'cause' to one of the 'risks' of poverty. But Townsend provides information on these risks too. The characteristics associated with either a very low or a very high risk of poverty are listed in descending order (Townsend 1979: 896. Table 26.1). These are given in great detail, forty-two in all being listed. According to Townsend's relative deprivation standard, those who run the highest risk of being in poverty are:

1. those in a household of a man, woman and three or more children, where the occupational status is that of unskilled manual worker (93 per cent of this group were in poverty)
2. being aged 80 years or over (82%)
3. having an appreciable or severe disability and being of pensionable age (82%)
4. being a child (aged 0– 14 years) with parents of unskilled manual status (77%)
5. having an appreciable or severe disability (74%)
6. being retired or living alone and aged 60 years or more (70%).

The factors Townsend found to be associated with poverty are the familiar ones: unskilled manual work; old age; disability; childhood; fatherless or single-parent families; few years of education; unemployment. It is worth noting that he also found that almost half of people who were 'non-white' were relatively deprived (42% compared to 26% for all those in the sample). Townsend concludes that the risks of poverty are highly correlated with occupation, with employment status and with dependency. It is this dependency status which increases the risks with age. In addition, he found that a higher proportion than is officially believed of those in poverty or on the margins of poverty are not at any single time receiving means-tested benefits.

Although these findings date from the late sixties, they cannot be said to overstate the problem. During the seventies, unemployment increased and so did the proportion of elderly people and the number of single-parent families. About half the population experience poverty at some point in their lives, especially those who are manual workers, women or the disabled and children in families dependent on such people. If the experience of poverty relates to sympathy for the poor, and with political identification of their needs, then it may be that the scope for radical reform is greater than is often assumed.

LOW WAGES

One factor contributing to the problem of poverty is that of low pay. We have already seen that low pay is the main cause of the poverty of 17 per cent of those who live below the supplementary benefit level. Low pay also contributes to the hardship experienced by the millions living at or just above the poverty line. However, low pay influences poverty indirectly. There are two important ways in which this occurs. First, low pay at one time may contribute to poverty later in life. This is most clearly demonstrated by poverty in old age. Low pay during working life prevents the acquisition of property, particularly home-ownership, rights in an occupational pension scheme and the accumulation of savings. Second, what was referred to earlier as being on the edges of the labour market relates to low pay. Low-paid workers are more likely to become unemployed, they are less likely to enjoy fringe benefits, such as sick pay schemes, and their employment is less secure. Low-paid workers are principally manual workers (4/5 of all low-paid workers). Twenty per cent work in industry and 16 per cent are farm or service workers. The relationship of the poor to the State is a complex one. The majority are dependent on State welfare benefits for their income. A large proportion of those whose earnings are low, who stand on the edges of poverty, are likely to be employed in the public sector, particularly in services and distribution. Of course, low-paid workers are found also in private industry, especially in the hotel and catering trade (N.B.P.I. 1971). Inadequate life-time earnings, job insecurity, sickness and ill-health correlate with low pay and contribute to poverty.

Low pay must be seen more generally as a disadvantage in the labour market, and as associated with high incidence of job instability and ill-health and with the absence of fringe benefits. The low-paid worker is more vulnerable to the interruption or loss of earning power, and lacks the resources to meet such needs ... poverty is often viewed as something which could happen to anyone – either as a result of bad luck (losing one's job or becoming sick) or on account of the natural process of growing old. Related to this is the belief that much poverty is transitory, that (it) is a temporary disruption or one associated with one particular stage of the life-cycle. This view, however, is highly misleading ... low pay is a thread which runs throughout people's working lifetime and beyond into retirement, and what may appear at first sight to be 'bad luck' is likely to be related to labour market disadvantage. Poverty does not happen to just anyone. (Atkinson 1973: 116–17)

INEQUALITY AND POVERTY

It has sometimes been argued that, since the proportion of the population found to live in poverty remains constant, poverty at a minimal level of, say, 5 per cent is ineradicable. Poverty and the poor are always with us. Such explanations of the inevitability of poverty tend to refer to the characteristics of the 'residuum' (what might now be called the 'scum'), characteristics which lead to their rejection by society, their inability to 'fit in' or 'match up' to the demands of society. The poor are those who 'cannot cope', are unable to 'function adequately' in society. They should be treated as dependents and as the objects of charity.

These views also tend to emphasise the rise in the standard of living of the lowest groups over time, consistent with a general rise in the prosperity of society. They minimize the hardship experienced by the poor, viewing poverty as the condition of a category rather than as the experience of people in society. If being poor is viewed differently, as something which happens to people, the implication is that poverty refers to a relationship between people in society. There can be no 'poor' without there being others who are 'rich'. When people see themselves as poor, when others treat them differently because they are poor, when events in their lives are dictated by their lowly social position, poverty is then not just an abstract concept but a real experience. But poverty is neither inevitable nor ineradicable. It is the result of decisions taken by people and it could be altered by their actions.

One element in the process by which poverty is directly linked to inequality is that of the arrangements for financing social security benefits. Those who are poor are predominantly either low wage-earners or the unemployed. Low wages contribute doubly to the problem, both directly, where wages and conditions of employment are inadequate, particularly when lifetime income is considered, and indirectly since social security levels of benefit are set in relation to them. Those who are outside the labour market and dependent on social security are dependent on the contributions made by those who are employed, through taxation and national insurance. Since social security benefits are financed out of the earnings of the occupied population, they are integrally related to the level of earnings provided by the labour market. Raising social security benefits to an adequate level would depend on overcoming obstacles in the way of increasing the total revenue provided through taxation and national insurance contributions. It could also be done by altering the distribution of these revenues between the various categories of State expenditure (for example, by cutting expenditure on armaments or the monarchy to increase expenditure on welfare). The first point involves the issue of resistance to further deductions from income, that is, to a lowering of the standard of living of some to improve that of the poor. At present, the system of financing social security results largely in a horizontal redistribution from the 'occupied' to the 'unoccupied' members of the labour force, that is, principally from those in middle years to the young and the old, and from the employed to the unemployed. An alternative form of redistribution would be a vertical redistribution, improving the standard of living of the poor by reducing that of the well-off or rich. To evaluate this issue, it is necessary to consider the distribution of income and wealth in modern Britain.

The Royal Commission on the Distribution of Income and Wealth in its *Initial Report* concluded that 'the top half of income recipients ... received just over three quarters (i.e. 76%) of total income; the bottom half received just under a quarter (i.e. 24%) of total income. The top 20 per cent had more than seven times the share in total income of the bottom 20 per cent (42.7% against 5.8%). The top 10 per cent and the bottom half each received about one quarter of total income (i.e. 26% and 24% respectively).' (Report No. 1. 1975: para. 318) Discussing the impact of progressive income tax, the Commission concludes that this had some effect but that the shift was relatively small. 'In 1972/3 taxation reduced the share of the top 10 per cent from 26.9 per cent to 23.6 per cent and increased the share of the bottom 20 per cent from 5.8 per cent to 6.8 per cent.' (op. cit.: para. 320) They concluded 'the main forces in the redistribution of income are transfer payments, upon which many households lower down the distribution are partially or entirely dependent and direct taxes which effect a proportionately greater reduction in the incomes of those higher up the distribution ... However, taxes on expenditure are broadly regressive and can be shown to offset to a large extent, the redistributive effect of taxes on income. Alternatively, the progressive effect of benefits in kind from the social services on the distribution can be shown as largely offset by the incidence of indirect taxation.' (op. cit.: para. 321) Finally, as regards any consistent trend towards greater equality in the distribution of incomes, the Commission concluded that there was little evidence of any move in that direction. 'It is between 1938 and 1949 that the biggest change occurred in the income distribution. The share of the top one per cent fell by over a third and that of the top 10 per cent by over a fifth.' (op. cit.: para. 322).

The findings of the Commission on the distribution of wealth are that personal wealth is very much less evenly distributed than personal income. In 1973, the latest year for which they had estimates available, more than a quarter of all personal wealth was owned by the richest 1 per cent of the adult population and about a half of all the wealth was owned by the richest 5 per cent; and two-thirds of all personal wealth was owned by the richest 10 per cent.

These conclusions may seem inconsistent with the popular belief that the distribution of incomes in post-war years has been moving clearly in the direction of equality. This 'tendency' has been attributed to the egalitarian effects of social and economic policy, full employment and the disappearance of the wealthy. For example, in 1972, the Inland Revenue Department itself concluded that 'the broad picture of the last 20 years is of a tendency for variations between incomes to diminish' (*Survey of Personal Incomes 1969–70*). If one looks at the figures more closely, however, one sees that, although there has been some loss by the top group, there has been no corresponding gain by the bottom group. The two factors which account for what trend towards egalitarianism has occurred are, first, the achievement of full employment in earlier post-war years and, second, the increase in the employment of married women, which has raised the household income of those families where both adults are employed.

Townsend's study also brings out the extent of inequality and deprivation at work. A quarter of the men interviewed had worked 50 or more hours in the previous week. Forty-four per cent of men (and 51 per cent of women) were subject to one week's notice or less. Thirty-seven per cent of men received no wages or salary during sickness from their employer. Fifty-six per cent had paid holidays of two weeks or less. And 43 per cent of men (61 per cent of women) had no entitlement to an occupational pension. These conditions were more likely to be found among unskilled manual workers. For example, only 9 per cent of unskilled manual workers had two weeks paid holiday per year whereas this was the case for 59 per cent of those with a professional or managerial occupation. A quarter of unskilled manual workers were entitled to an occupational pension whereas almost all (96 per cent) professional or managerial workers were. Seventy-seven per cent of unskilled manual workers were subject to one week's notice or less whereas this was the case for only 4 per cent of the professional or managerial group.

CONCLUSION

All these facts and figures may seem hard to digest but they add up to the same conclusions: the continuance of poverty in spite of affluence; the very high risk of poverty in old age; the likelihood of poverty in single-parent families, in families where a woman is the head, where the head is an unskilled manual worker or receiving low wages. Dependence on social security benefits in general means living in poverty. At the same time, the richest 1 per cent in the UK own at least 20 per cent of all personal wealth. The richest 1 per cent receive the same amount of income as the poorest 20 per cent. Whatever the causes, explanations and justifications might be, it seems clear that in spite of the Welfare State, Britain remains a profoundly unequal society.

What emerges from this consideration of the evidence on 'who are the poor' in post-war Britain is that the 'facts' do not speak clearly for themselves. Apart from the serious technical difficulties involved in the collection and analysis of data, differences instantly appear as soon as interpretation of the statistics begins. Primarily, the definition of poverty used affects conclusions regarding the number in poverty at any one time and trends over time. However, where the most stringent definition is used, that is those living below the poverty line (defined using contemporary supplementary benefit scales), it is indisputable that poverty remains a significant social problem, affecting the lives of at least 2.5 million people at any one time. Some see these 2.5 million as only the tip of the iceberg. A much larger number of people experience poverty at some time in their lives or experience poverty in some but not all areas of their lives. Depending on one's perspective, definition of poverty and methods of measurement, between 2.5 million and 10 million people constitute the poor and needy in British society.

We may wish to discount the extreme variation between the income of the destitute tramp under Waterloo Bridge and that of the man at the top (like the highest-paid man in Britain, reputed to be the chairman of S. & W. Berisford, the sugar importers, who receives a gross salary of £272,672 a year, and who incidentally got a rise of £1,155 a week from the first Conservative budget in 1979). However, the range of variation between the top executive and the agricultural worker is 50 : 1 (Atkinson 1975: 19). The difference between the incomes of the top 20 per cent and the bottom 20 per cent is 7 : 1. Now, it should be recalled that the difference between the income of the man in the middle and the level of supplementary benefits has been of the order of 2 : 1 in the post-war years. It is patently clear that it would be wrong to argue that social security levels should be raised to two-thirds of average incomes, a level which would provide a reasonable income and eliminate most poverty, without placing this aim within a larger programme of reform. Not only would it be wrong but it would be resisted fiercely by the man in the middle. The blinkered view which dominated the post-war years tried to deal with the problems of poverty and insecurity simply through an overall increase in levels of taxation and national insurance contributions. This has now reached its limits and has clearly failed to deal satisfactorily with the problem. The only possibility of solution lies with an integrated programme of reforms which would include a reappraisal of taxation and national insurance within an all-embracing incomes policy aimed at vertical redistribution of income.

Part two
RECENT HISTORY OF THE ISSUE

Chapter four
CONCEPTS OF POVERTY

The academic debate about poverty has been largely about definitions. None of these social scientists, however, is an 'ivory-tower intellectual'. Most have been involved in one way or another in the 'real world of politics'. But the effect of all their labour has often been minimal or at least different from what they intended.

Poverty has always had several not entirely separable meanings and it is always defined according to the conventions of the society in which it occurs. (Eric Hobsbawm 1968)

The empirical tradition in the social sciences attempts to provide an alternative to dogmatic explanations of social behaviour by testing commonsense assumptions about social life. However, major criticisms have been made of this approach. Many so-called 'value-free' definitions turn out to be not only influenced by their social context, but also to be permeated by social and moral judgements. In looking at the common definitions of poverty it is thus important to see how far they reflect competing ideologies.

One major concern of the empirical tradition in British sociology has been with the problem of poverty. Social investigators assume that it is possible to define poverty as a distinct social problem and propose solutions based on an assessment of its causes and conditions. The approach is set within a reformist tradition.

In looking at differing definitions of poverty, the point is to see whose definitions prevail, where and in what ways they have been influential; in particular, to see how successful the attempt to define poverty objectively has been and whether this has had any impact on social policy. Although we are mainly concerned with developments in post-war Britain, it is useful to sketch in the background by looking at changes over the past century – and the bald conclusion is that in spite of the obvious changes in the standard of living and in styles of life, views on poverty are remarkably intransigent. The Poor Law and Victorian attitudes die hard.

There is a sense in which in an unequal society the poor will always be with us; but it is a separate question why poverty continues in a relatively rich society. Charles Booth's selection of 'poverty' rather than 'the poor' as a subject for investigation one hundred years ago marked a highly significant turning point in British social thought. He invented the concept of 'the poverty line' and the ideas of 'living above the line' of poverty or 'on the line'.

By the word 'poor', I mean to describe those who have a fairly regular though bare income, such as 18 shillings or 21 shillings per week for the moderate family, and by the 'very poor' those who fall below this standard, whether from chronic irregularity of work, sickness, or a large number of young children. I do not here introduce any moral question: whatever the cause, those whose means prove to be barely sufficient or quite insufficient for decent independent life, are counted as 'poor' or 'very poor' respectively: and as it is not always possible to ascertain the exact income, the classification is also based on the appearance of the home. (Booth 1887 quoted in Simey and Simey 1960:184)

Booth was criticised for his attempt to define the poverty line. The criticisms were of three kinds: first, that the level at which the poverty line was set – 18 shillings – was a perfectly adequate income; second, regarding the reliability of information, there were said to be many cases of undisclosed earnings; and third, that if people were poor this was because they were extravagant in their spending. Professor Levi, for example, took the view that 'poverty proper in the Tower Hamlets was more frequently produced by vice, extravagance and waste, or by unfitness for work, the result in many cases of immoral habits, than by real want of employment or low wages' (Simey and Simey 1960:184). In the 1870s and early 1880s the poor were commonly viewed as unregenerate, as those who had turned their back on progress or had been rejected by it. They were 'the residuum'. The eminent and influential economist Marshall, for example, saw them as 'those who have a poor physique and a weak character – those who are limp in body and mind' (Stedman Jones 1971:11). As Stedman Jones comments, 'the problem was not structural but moral. The evil to be combated was not poverty but pauperism: pauperism with its attendant vices, drunkenness, improvidence, mendicancy, bad language, filthy habits, gambling, low amusements, and ignorance.' (ibid.)

The distinction between the poor and the pauper is still evident today. We talk about those with low incomes as different from those dependent on supplementary benefits. A variety of remedies have become accepted, like old-age pensions and unemployment and sickness insurance, to deal with the problems of some of the poor, those seen as the 'deserving'. However, those seen as 'undeserving' remain set apart as outcasts and their 'dependency' is seen as having mainly to do with their 'inadequacy' (our contemporary term for being 'limp in body and mind').

In arguments about poverty today, there is implicit reference to the distinction between the categories of the 'poor' and the 'pauper': Where people decry the fact, for example, that some of the 'poor' have incomes lower than the level set for supplementary benefit, i.e. for paupers; or where it is said that some of the low-paid receive less in work than out of work; or where it is shown that some of the old will not claim benefits because they do not wish to be stigmatised as paupers or objects of charity. The distinction is used when it is argued that some of those who have to live on supplementary benefits are forced to do so because of social circumstances rather than because of their laziness or moral weakness. It is argued, for example, that lone parents with responsibility for small children are forced to rely on supplementary benefit through no fault of their own and should instead be given a social benefit as of right. In all these discussions a distinction is being made between the poor (there because of social circumstances) and the pauper (there because of habits and attitudes). Although the term 'pauper' may not be used, the idea remains. These arguments are often about the way the two categories have become confused or are not sufficiently sharply demarcated, or how some people have been wrongly categorised. The validity of the distinction is rarely questioned.

The two most common views in Victorian times, against which Booth tried to argue, saw poverty as resulting either from laziness and indolence (thought to be a natural tendency of mankind and one which would be encouraged by the actions of sentimental philanthropists) or from vice, especially the Demon Drink. Booth attempted to show that poverty was a social condition that might arise for a large number of reasons, of which idleness and vice were only two, and that drink might be the result rather than the cause of poverty. Clearly over the century more recognition has been given to the contribution of social conditions to poverty. However, since there has also been a growth in social benefits, what poverty remains is commonly explained as the result of indolence and vice. A reading of the arguments about 'scrounging' which have become prominent in Britain since 1976, immediately and easily indicates the resilience of Victorian attitudes.

The attempt to discuss poverty objectively and without prejudice has thus had only limited success. Booth himself, especially in his proposals on how to deal with the lowest groups, exhibited many of the prejudices of his time (Class A, the lowest group, should be harried out of existence; and for Class B, the next above, a strict regime in labour colonies where they would become servants of the State, was suggested).

However, the idea of a poverty line has been influential because it was incorporated into social legislation. The Beveridge Report was particularly important here with its emphasis on the need for a subsistence minimum for rates of benefit. Since then, discussion of poverty in Britain has been taken up with the issue of how to define an 'adequate' income. This discussion has mainly been conducted by academics, social workers, and civil servants although it has extended at times to the political parties. A large proportion of the public too seem to think of poverty in terms of subsistence. In Townsend's survey, 31 per cent described poverty in this way and a further 29 per cent seemed to have this in mind in describing the minority groups who were living in poverty (Townsend, 1979: 240).

But what is meant by 'subsistence'? In Townsend's survey, those who described poverty in these terms 'spoke of not having enough to feed children or to go to work on; having nothing to wear or threadbare clothing; and not having the basic necessities of life' (op. cit: 238). Townsend comments that: 'The conception of a necessary minimum income lurked in these accounts and the emphasis was principally upon the physical necessities of food, clothing and shelter.' People spoke of 'living in slum conditions; not enough money for the essentials of life ... It's not having enough food and clothes and being behind with the rent and not being able to pull up ... I suppose it's simply being short of the necessaries of life – living hand to mouth and perhaps going without food and clothes.' – (idem.)

In trying to define a poverty line, how should one decide what are the minimum necessaries in present-day society? In measuring whether people have enough to meet necessary obligations, how should one decide what resources to take into account? Technical questions of what information to use and how reliable it is need not concern us at the moment. The issue is whether it is possible to agree on a definition of the resources required for 'subsistence' in modern-day Britain.

The subsistence definition of poverty derives from that formulated by Seebohm Rowntree in the first of his famous studies of York in the years 1899, 1936 and 1950. The main elements in his definition were income and food consumption. A family would be considered to be living in poverty if its 'total earnings are insufficient to obtain the minimum necessaries for the maintenance of merely physical efficiency' (Rowntree 1901:86). In this 'basket of goods' view, nutritional requirements are translated into quantities of food to which a cash value is attributed, and the rent paid and minimum amounts for clothing and sundries are then added. This should provide a base-line from which to judge the amount of poverty in a society. Rowntree, however, recognised that the definition of subsistence changes over time. In his later studies, in 1936 and 1950, he provided a longer list of the 'minimum necessaries', allowing for cultural and historical changes. Families below the poverty line would always be undernourished, but those above the line could get by–if they were careful with their money. This was Rowntree's distinction between primary and secondary poverty. Primary poverty, where minimal nutritional standards were not met because of an insufficiency of resources, was caused by inadequate income. Secondary poverty occurred where resources, in themselves sufficient, were not utilised rationally. Here the cause of poverty lay in the irrational behaviour of the poor, their unwise spending patterns.

In preparing his Report in 1942, Beveridge went to great lengths to calculate in minute detail the resources which would be required to provide a basic existence. In fact, Rowntree was an expert witness to his Committee. His calculations were based on the judgements of nutritionists of what was required to provide an adequate diet and on the views of other experts on basic clothing and other expenses. Housing, clothing and food, with a very small amount added for other expenses, were the basic needs considered in these calculations. In spite of this, the post-war legislation set the standard of national insurance benefits lower than Beveridge's extremely low limit. Due largely to the activities of the poverty lobby, benefit rates have been raised periodically in post-war years so that the level has on the whole kept pace with rises in the general standard of living. Although the position of the poor relative to the average has remained the same, the standard of living used to define poverty has risen in real terms over these years.

Some have used this fact to argue that the poverty line is now meaningless: that it no longer defines poverty in terms of subsistence but simply represents the level of income regarded as tolerable by the rest of society for those who are dependent on state benefits. Poverty, they say, as Booth, Rowntree and Beveridge conceived it (in terms of subsistence), is no longer measured by the official poverty line (the supplementary benefit level) since this income can buy more than the minimum necessaries. Real poverty is no longer a major problem, they claim. Those who are destitute, the down-and-outs, the dossers and the vagrants, are a tiny proportion of the population and remain there mainly because of individual problems such as alcoholism, drug addiction, or mental illness. The remainder of those living on supplementary benefit, or with low incomes, although poor relative to others in society, cannot be considered to be living in poverty. They are neither starving nor destitute nor in want. Their basic needs can be satisfied, if they are careful with their money, although they may be deprived of many of the pleasures that others can afford. This is not a matter of poverty but of inequality.

How then do others argue that poverty remains in present-day Britain? Can we talk of a poverty line and is the level set by supplementary benefits the one to use?

The issue can be clarified by listing basic needs for men, women and children in our society in much the same way as Rowntree and Booth assessed what was required for decent and independent existence by a working man and his family in their Victorian society. What income and other resources are necessary for a man to be able to pay his way in the circumstances in which a working man finds himself today?

Supplementary benefit rates aim to assess just that:

The scale-rates are regarded by the Commission as covering all normal needs that can be foreseen, including food, fuel and light, the normal repair and replacement of clothing, household sundries (but not major items of bedding and furnishing) and provision for amenities such as newspapers, entertainments and television licences. (SBC *Handbook*, Feb. 1977: para. 43)

The supplementary benefit rates from November 1980 are:

Husband and wife (short term)	£34.60
Husband and wife (long term)	£43.45
Person alone (short-term)	£21.30
Person alone (long-term)	£27.15

Non-householder age 18+ (short-term)	£17.05
Non-householder age 18+ (long-term)	£21.70
Non-householder age 16–17 (short-term)	£13.10
Non-householder age 16–17 (long-term)	£16.65
Dependent children age 11–15	£10.90
Dependent children up to 10 years	£ 7.30

The income provided through supplementary benefit in 1980 is one which would be considerably higher than that required for subsistence by a Victorian labourer or an Indian peasant but inadequate to meet the needs of an American city ghetto-dweller. But behaviour is socially conditioned and there are rules of behaviour, informal and formal, which must be observed if a man is to make his way in the society in which he finds himself. A man turning up for interview for a factory job dressed like a Victorian labourer, would be unlikely to be employed. He would probably be judged to be a tramp and thus unreliable. But all new needs do not represent simply a change in styles of living or a rise in the quality of life. Surveys constantly show (and the experience of teachers and social workers confirms) that there are still people in Britain today who have neither enough to eat nor sufficient clothing, who do not have adequate furniture or other household equipment. Being in poverty in Britain today means things like going without food in order to pay the electricity bill or having only one pair of shoes and no overcoat. These are not just matters of doing without a few luxuries. They refer to basic needs in our society.

In Townsend's classic study (1979), a whole chapter is devoted to The Impact of Poverty. It sets out the case-histories of some of those interviewed, from which a few quotations give an indication of the pathetic lives there described

Because the family cannot afford new glass, the room gets too cold and the boys sleep in one bedroom (:305). (This is the family of a disabled man, severely epileptic, whose family are all in bad health.) They go to bed early to save fuel. Mrs. Nelson buys second-hand clothing at jumble sales. For breakfast, she cooks porridge for the children but she and her husband have nothing. They are used to days without any cooked meal (:308). The furniture – 'everything in here, except the TV, which we rent, has been given to us' (:309). 'Had the family had a summer holiday recently?' 'Oh, yes' said Mrs Nelson immediately, 'we saved and saved for weeks. We put the money in that pot up there. Mind you, we had to take it out sometimes but we managed to put it back. Then the time came and we really did go together to see *The Sound of Music*. Oh, it was lovely – that opening scene when she was dancing on the mountains and all free. The children each had an ice-cream and when we left we walked up the High Street and you know that wallpaper shop, well, we saw that picture there, above our fireplace. We counted up our money. If we walked home we would just have enough for it. So next morning, I walked down and bought it and there it's been ever since. When you're fed up you can look at it and it reminds you of *The Sound of Music*.' Mr Nelson died in 1976. He was 43 (:310).

Describing the house of a long-term unemployed man with a wife and six children:

The house was the worst the interviewer had ever seen in his life. It consists of four small rooms and a tiny kitchen. There is a WC in the yard outside, no bath and no cooker. There is a cold tap but no wash basin or sink. It has every structural problem imaginable. Even with a coal fire in the back room it is cold. The roof leaks, there is loose brickwork and plaster and decaying floorboards. The doors fit badly, the plaster is cracked. When the back door is closed, the vibration causes other doors to open. The larder is of rough stone, which is black and cold. There are said to be rats, mice, bugs and cockroaches. The rat catcher came a few weeks ago when, after demolition started near by, the number of vermin increased, but said he could not put poison down because of the danger to the children. Upstairs, both bedrooms are cold and damp. The wallpaper is peeling. The ceiling is giving way and they have stuck paper over it to delay a fall. Beds have to be covered with plastic sheets to keep the damp off them. In one bedroom, husband and wife sleep with the two youngest daughters. In the other, two sons sleep in one double bed and two older daughters in another. The carpets downstairs have to be kept rolled up because of the damp. Mr and Mrs Mulligan are fearful of the house literally blowing down in a gale. The whole environment is dismal. The house next door is empty and in an advanced state of dilapidation. Tramps sleep there. The air in the neighbourhood is so smoky 'it looks as if a big fire is always burning'. The children have nowhere to play indoors and nowhere safe nearby. (op. cit.: 314)

How is it that such conditions continue to exist? Partly it is because the rates laid down for supplementary benefits are inadequate, particularly regarding the cost of children; partly because the income they provide is insufficient to maintain existence over a long time, being designed for short-term needs only (this affects especially the long-term unemployed and their families); partly because individual circumstances and needs vary, for example, certain illnesses require special diets; or some people have to spend more on travelling or heating than the supplementary benefit rates allow. Even where rates are adequate, not everyone gets what they are entitled to because mistakes can be made by officers at local social security offices, who are human like the rest of us, and often overworked, so that delays in payments occur. But in other cases, what has happened is not only that new needs have arisen with social change, but that the amount of control people have over their lives and thus over their expenditure has been reduced. Where a family live in a remote area without adequate public transport, a car may be a necessity. With the decline of the local shop, where perhaps credit could be arranged and small measures of things purchased, more expensive packaged goods have to be bought at the supermarket. A well-acknowledged change is that of the increasing distance and cost of the journey to work. Where families live in high-rise blocks where they cannot control the central heating, they do not have the choice to switch to a cheaper form of heating, like paraffin heating, when short of money. A television may be a basic need for a young mother with small children living in a council flat, on an estate without adequate playing areas, where, for example, notices order children not to play football on the grass or ride bicycles. There are innumerable examples of cases where the costs of subsistence, in terms of survival in modern circumstances, have risen above the level provided by supplementary benefits without a parallel rise in the standard of living; where people say they are barely 'existing', let alone 'living'.

To bring out these cases and to refute the view that poverty is a thing of the past, it would be helpful to have a clear and acceptable poverty line defined in terms of subsistence – the basic needs that must be satisfied for existence in present-day circumstances. One would be talking about the needs of workers, householders and school-children, the basic social roles, without having to go into the niceties of what is required to act as a good neighbour or citizen.

David Piachaud, in his pamphlet 'The Cost of a Child' (1979), has made a start in this direction by drawing up lists of what children need at various ages up to eleven and calculating the cost. This turned out to be about 50 per cent more than the amounts allowed for children in families on supplementary benefit (and on average more than twice what working parents get in child benefit). In calculating the 'modern minimum', Piachaud accepted that 'there is no such thing as a rational, scientific or objective basis for deciding what a child requires'. His assessment used a low-cost diet based on an American study of nutritional needs, clothing requirements arrived at by talking to mothers (and in most cases reducing their estimates), and modest allowances for household goods, heating and lighting, a week at Butlin's and a number of other conventional necessities. The result was a very frugal definition of a modern minimum. The point is that even this very low level was well above that provided by supplementary benefits.

Thus, if we use the supplementary benefit level as our poverty line we will be underestimating the extent of poverty. But as we have seen, even using this measure, there is no doubt that 'real poverty' has not yet been eliminated from our society. What is badly needed at present is a new poverty line developing further Piachaud's work, one perhaps constructed in a way similar to that put forward by Dudley Jackson and other economists. Jackson's definition shares the basic assumptions of Rowntree's subsistence view but is more refined (Jackson 1972). 'When important needs are not met, individuals or families are said to be in poverty because the condition of their lives is not considered satisfactory.' (op. cit.: 13) Jackson points out that the problem of defining poverty is largely one of defining what is or is not to count as 'adequate social functioning'. Social functioning, he argues, depends upon the fulfilment of needs: to function adequately in contemporary society, not only an individual's nutritional needs but also his need for education, housing and security must be met. Nutritional needs are satisfactorily met if they offer an individual the life-expectancy which is the standard in that society. 'Failure to realise that the "minimum" nutritional flow is related to a standard of health – which can approximately be measured by life-expectancy – has caused much confusion in the discussion of want.' (Jackson 1972: 16) Failure to meet nutritional needs satisfactorily constitutes *want*. However, social functioning in contemporary society depends not only on reaching the required standard of physical health, but also upon the ability to be employed, maintain a family and participate in social life. Failure to provide adequately for such needs in society constitutes *deprivation*. *Deprivation plus want together make up poverty*. Whereas in the conventional subsistence definition there is a tacit and rather reluctant recognition of 'cultural' and 'social' variables, here the need for adequate education, housing and security is firmly established as integral to the definition of poverty.

In relating his definition of 'adequate' nutritional resources to the standard expectation of life in a society, Jackson usefully emphasises the continuing problem of 'want'. In addition, a recognition of the importance of needs other than simply nutritional ones, consideration of whether an individual has a share in the educational, employment or housing stocks of his country, can provide an objective indicator of the extent of poverty. The implication is that poverty is not just the particular problem of a limited and defined section of society, but is integrally related to conditions in society as a whole. Discussion of poverty has to consider the manner in which resources are allocated and distributed. It is important to recognise also the way in which needs and their fulfilment are inter-related. Deprivation in one sphere is likely to produce deprivation in another: those who acquire assets of education are more likely to have more security and better housing; those with poor health are likely to suffer deprivation in other spheres, such as employment and security.

Poverty is seen here as a lack of human capital. Modern society is viewed as a market in which individuals compete for a share of total resources. An individual's ability to compete is determined by his assets, which are not only financial but include, especially, skills and education. Social and economic changes, for example technological change and urbanisation, involve changes in the definition of needs. Not only does the definition of an 'acceptable' level of living change over time but survival and adequate functioning require the satisfaction of new needs which do not necessarily constitute an improvement in social conditions. Examples here might be the costs of the journey to work or the demand for literacy and numeracy for adequate functioning as a worker or consumer. This is an important critique of the complacent view that progress is inherent in industrial development: 'economic growth provides no guarantee that poverty will disappear. As the economy grows, it grows in complexity and sophistication and so makes greater demands on the individual.' (Jackson 1972: 18) A further implication is that the surplus produced by economic growth is not necessarily used to alleviate poverty. There may be less choice than some supposed about the distribution of any extra revenue. The systems of production and exchange may require a certain allocation of resources which may do little or nothing to reduce poverty or increase welfare. If the increasing complexity of the economy makes demands on the individual which some are unable to meet, those who do not acquire the necessary skills will be marginal to the labour force and suffer deprivation in other spheres too.

This view of the effects of economic growth has, however, been challenged, notably by Bravermann in *Labour and Monopoly Capital* (1974) who questions the extent to which an increasingly skilled labour force is being produced or is required. Even so, it is worth noting that a more sophisticated definition of poverty involves the recognition that poverty cannot be considered in isolation from the rest of society, in particular from the systems of distribution and production.

Most 'relative' concepts of poverty add to the list of resources required for adequate functioning in society. In particular, sociologists have emphasised the need to include *status* and *power* as relevant resources. They concentrate on the distribution of resources, in particular differences in the opportunities available. They say individuals do not compete on equal terms. The concepts which are introduced in these alternative perspectives are: multiple deprivation, life-style, status, stigma, integration, power, consciousness, apathy and despair. Policies and solutions proposed relate to the questions, how can the distribution of resources or opportunities be made more equal? and how far should this process go?

These arguments have had great influence on discussions of poverty. They arose as part of a radical critique which aimed to demonstrate that poverty continues to be the experience of large numbers of people in modern Britain and continues to be a social problem despite post-war social legislation. Criticism were made of the inadequacy of provision, especially the low level set as the 'minimum adequate to the maintenance of an acceptable way of life'. It was argued not only that the cash levels of supplementary benefit scales needed to be improved but also better provision of other services, in housing, health and education was required were poverty ever to be abolished.

The most important post-war exponent of this view, whose teachings and writings inspired a number of followers, was the late Richard M. Titmuss, formerly Professor of Social Administration at the London School of Economics. Social services he considered to be not society's 'ambulance wagons' (in Lloyd George's phrase) nor its 'safety-net' (in Churchill's) but an organic part and mirror of the society which provided them. They could and should be the instruments of profound social change. The purpose here was not to provide an objective, value-free definition of poverty but, through the study of poverty, to offer a moral critique of and new public standards for British society.

Peter Townsend and Brian Abel-Smith were taught and influenced by Titmuss. Peter Townsend began his studies of poverty to demonstrate the persistence of poverty in affluent, post-war Britain. He aimed also to construct a sociological definition of poverty, which would be sensitive to the experience of being poor and would allow comparisons to be made over time and between social groups and societies. His views have changed somewhat over the years, but his most recent definition of poverty argues that

Poverty can be defined objectively and applied consistently only in terms of the concept of relative deprivation ... Individuals, families and groups in the population can be said to be in poverty when they lack the resources to obtain the type of diet, participate in the activities and have the living conditions and amenities which are customary or at least widely encouraged or approved, in the societies to which they belong. Their resources are so seriously below those commanded by the average individual or family that they are, in effect, excluded from ordinary living patterns, customs and activities. (Townsend 1979: 31)

Factors other than food and income must be included, such as resources and life-style. It is particularly the emphasis on life-style that distinguishes Townsend's definition from the human capital definition, together with the stress placed on a lack of resources at a number of levels, echoing Titmuss in emphasising the importance not only of income but also of capital, benefits in kind, fringe benefits (for example, pension rights), job security, working conditions and so on, plus the components of what has come to be known as the 'social wage', use of and access to public property and services. The complexity of this definition, which makes it preferable conceptually to the official or conventional versions, raises problems, however, regarding its usefulness, in that it is much more difficult to operationalise either for measurement or as a basis for policy and practice (viz., the length of time required to complete *Poverty in the United Kingdom*). The implication of Townsend's definition (which is more important as a critical tool than as a precise measuring rod) is that the extent of poverty is greater than officially or commonly supposed. There are problems with this definition, however, not least the question of what constitutes 'the style of living customary to the average'. And is not the level at which resources are 'seriously below the average' the very point where a poverty line could be drawn?

The concepts to which poverty as relative deprivation are linked are those of citizenship, justice, social solidarity and cohesion. The key element stressed by Townsend is that of 'participation'. Because of a lack of resources, individuals and groups are further deprived of the chance to fully participate in society. They become outsiders, they are not fully integrated, and are in effect deprived of their rights as citizens. A barrier is built up between those in poverty and those not, which acts to reinforce the divide. Critical problems are those of isolation and lack of power, which prevent individuals or groups from sharing in the activities of society as a whole. To some extent this perspective shifts the emphasis from the experience of physical hardship to the experience of not being wanted, of being abandoned, being treated differently and as inferior. It does therefore tend to neglect the question whether physical hardship and material deprivation continue to exist and which is the greater problem, which a subsistence definition places squarely at the centre of the argument. The isolation of the poor is a problem for society, too, in that it leads to fragmentation, a lack of cohesion and integration. The continuance of poverty, defined as relative deprivation, is a moral problem in that it denies the value of certain individuals to society; it is unjust and unfair. In spite of its obvious disadvantages, this conceptualisation is useful in that the poor are seen not only as a *category* but as a *group*. However, Townsend is keen to stress the link between integration and resources; a lack of resources leads to inability to fully participate in social life which in turn further reduces the resources available to that individual or group. The two elements are mutually reinforcing. In a sense, lack of resources is the *state* of being poor, inability to fully participate is the *process* through which poverty is experienced, continued and further developed. By contrast, an excess of resources is the state of being rich; extensive opportunities to participate (i.e. power and influence) are the process through which wealth is perpetuated and further developed. Townsend argues that his is an objective definition, less influenced by assumptions and prejudices than the apparently more simple subsistence definition, which is actually deeply imbued with prejudiced and ill-informed assumptions about working class life. 'Deprivation can arise in any or all of the major spheres of life – at work where the means largely determining one's position in other spheres are earned; at home, in neighbourhood and family; in travel; and in a range of social and individual activities outside work and home and neighbourhood. In principle there could be extreme divergencies in the experience of different kinds of deprivation. *In practice, there is a systematic relationship between deprivation and level of resources.*' (Townsend 1979: 915 – my italics)

In post-war years, the academic debate about poverty has been largely a debate about definitions. The conclusion must be, however, that the emphasis on the redefinition of poverty has been a disservice to the poor. In spite of good intentions, the strategy backfired. The notion of relative deprivation introduced by Peter Townsend and taken up by many in the poverty lobby confused the issue. Many people began to think that there was no longer any real poverty, that poverty was just a relative matter of whether one could afford a holiday in Spain or had to make do with Butlin's; or of whether or not one could afford to eat meat or might have to wear second-hand clothes – things which in themselves do not nowadays mark out a stigmatised and deprived group. Here Peter Townsend's contribution is crucial. His work has been so immense and varied that it is perhaps not surprising to find some confusion and inconsistency in his approach. In practice he has often continued to use a subsistence definition while theoretically he has promoted the concept of poverty as relative deprivation. An early valuable contribution was to tear to shreds the definition of subsistence used by Rowntree and Beveridge and incorporated into social policy, showing that it did not adequately meet basic needs and placed requirements on the poor for a saintliness of behaviour that would have been difficult for even one as puritanical as Beveridge himself to fulfil (Townsend 1954). He has continued to attack the mean and meagre view of people's need incorporated in existing social security provision. He argues that a new definition of subsistence should recognise people's social role in society and that their so-called irrational spending patterns do not reflect ignorance and defiant indulgence but social expectations. Subsistence involves maintaining the social body, not just the physical. We should abandon the physically lodged standard which rules today and recognise indicators of deprivation in other areas of life, especially those of work, housing and the community.

Townsend's insistence on seeing poverty as relative deprivation had the effect of draining the term poverty of its concrete, objective content and inadvertently contributed to the view that poverty no longer exists in our society. Why did he do this? Perhaps there was an element of sociological professionalism. Perhaps it was a rather naive attempt to introduce a discussion of inequality by the back door. He is undoubtedly, however, the foremost expert on poverty in Britain today and without his constant and unremitting efforts the plight of the poor would be even more neglected. Through his writings and practical political involvement, he has not let us forget that there exists an unreduced core of hardship and real poverty which could be ameliorated given moral commitment and political will.

The systematic nature of deprivation and the overlapping of disadvantages are emphasised in definitions which see poverty as multiple deprivation. Coates and Silburn (1973) comment that studies concerned with the specialist interests of poverty, poor housing, or inadequate schools each make valuable contributions to the growing debate on poverty and deprivation. 'People in the real world, however, cannot live such specialised lives, and it seems only too apparent that the family which lives its life in a Milner Holland slum may well do so in Abel-Smith/Townsend poverty while its children are sent to a Plowden school.' (Coates and Silburn 1973: 49– 50) In their study of an impoverished community, they try to show 'how all these different types of deprivation mesh one into another, to create for those who must endure them a total situation shot through and through by one level of want after another' (op. cit.: 50). They show how different forms of deprivation 'relate to one another, feed off one another, sustain and help to perpetuate one another' (ibid.). They show the overlapping and concentration of deprivation, each deprivation reinforcing and solidifying the gap between the poor and others. And, importantly, they raise the question of the relationship between the poor and the working class.

Clearly Townsend's view, and those of Titmuss, Coates and Silburn, is that poverty results from inequality in society. Others have argued that, because of this, poverty should not be considered separately from the question of inequality:

> The preoccupation with poverty is liable to obscure reality; and for that reason, in our view, it is on balance politically retrogressive in impact. In drawing an arbitrary line (or a series of lines) to distinguish the 'poor' from the rest, it diverts attention from the larger structure of inequality in which poverty so defined is embedded. That is often not the intention. On the contrary, much of the research on poverty – typically undertaken by radical rather than conservative social scientists – has started from an explicitly 'relative' definition of poverty. The 'poverty line' is set by reference to contemporary standards of expectation; it moves upwards over time as absolute levels of living improve; and it is acknowledged to be only one arbitrary line among many that could be drawn at different levels of the hierarchy of inequality. (Westergaard and Resler 1976: 123)

There are two risks, the authors argue, associated with this procedure. The first is *false diagnosis*, that is to attribute the causes of poverty to the characteristics of the poor, to individual conditions 'ostensibly unconnected with each other and unrelated, or only incidentally related, to class. The remedies often proposed are correspondingly discrete, directed to this or that particular condition by itself, whether they involve only financial assistance or also include measures of "prevention therapy". They are not designed to produce wholesale change in the general structure of inequality.' (op. cit.: 124) The second problem which follows from concentration on poverty rather than inequality is the encouraging of a distorted image of society. The poor are 'singled out from the mass of wage earners from which they are recruited. And the division is ignored between the wage-earning class – in or out of poverty – and the secure though differentiated ranks of the "middle and upper" classes.' (op. cit.: 125) This image runs the risk of 'false prescription', particularly in attributing the plight of the old-age pensioner or the low-paid to the actions of other wage earners rather than to the capital/labour relationship.

Although this critique is valid, its emphasis on the conflict between the 'middle and upper' classes and all those in 'the working class', overlooks the fundamental consideration of the very real differences in power, reward and perceived interests which exist between relatively secure and well-paid sections of organised labour and the low-paid and claimants.

J.C. Kincaid (1973) takes up this relationship in arguing that some are rich *because* some are poor.

'From the point of view of capitalism the low-wage sector helps to underpin and stabilise the whole structure of wages and the conditions of employment of the working class.' (:241)
   'It is immensely difficult for groups dependent on the welfare services to organise themselves in defence of their own interests or to agitate politically on welfare questions.' (:242)
   'The great weakness of groups dependent on the Welfare State is their isolation from and lack of links with the organised Labour movement which alone could have the strength to effect real changes in the structure of society.' (:244)

Ralph Miliband similarly emphasises the political dimension of the definition of poverty. Quoting with approval Coates and Silburn's view of poverty as having 'many dimensions, each of which must be studied separately but which in reality constitute an interrelated network of deprivations', he concerns himself with one element in this network of deprivations, one he considers to be crucial, the political element. 'The deprived not only lack economic resources, they also, and relatedly, lack political resources as well.' (Miliband 1974:183) He emphasises that an essential characteristic of those officially designated 'poor' is their class membership:

The tendency is to speak of the poor as the old; or as members of father-less families: or as the chronic sick and the disabled; or as the unemployed and their families; or as the low-paid. But old age, membership of father-less families, sickness and disablement, and even unemployment are not as such necessarily synonymous with poverty . . . Old age, disablement, low pay, unemployment, etc. become synonymous with poverty insofar as those involved are members of the working class – recruited, so to speak, from its ranks . . . The basic fact is that the poor are an integral part of the working class – its poorest and most disadvantaged stratum . . . Poverty is a class thing, closely linked to a *general* situation of class inequality. (op. cit.: 184– 5)

The aim of these studies is to emphasise the inevitability of pov-erty in 'capitalist' society. Poverty is the product of such societies and reformist measures can have only limited impact. The failure of social reform is not a failure of wills or of values; it is inevitable. Inequality is functional for the effectiveness of the economic sys-tem. Ironically, this view is shared by 'right-wing' supporters of the market system, such as Hayek, Milton Friedman, members of the Institute of Economic Affairs, Sir Keith Joseph, Mrs Thatcher and Sir Geoffrey Howe. The Right wing, however, claim that inequality is a good thing, for differential rewards act as incentives encouraging the acquisition of skills, hard work and risk – taking, on which everyone's prosperity depends. The Left, however, see inequality not as a hierarchy of individual differences but as part of a system of class relations. The values and practices referred to help to maintain the dominance of capital over labour, repressing and containing the power of the working class. Poverty is the corollary of the class structure: its definition and explanation cannot be divorced from analysis of that structure. This is a view now shared by Townsend who demonstrated in his recent monumental study that poverty is much more extensive than is generally recognised. His conclusion is that poverty is created by wealth. It is, he argues, rooted in the complex resource structure, principles of allocation of resources and social sponsorship of styles of living and not in indi-vidual capacities, minority adversity or community sub-cultures. If poverty is to be abolished or substantially reduced, the institutions and principles governing the allocation of resources and the promo-tion of styles of living need to be reconstructed. Mild redistributive social policies have become less effective and are thoroughly inade-quate (Townsend 1979: 892– 926).

The question remains, however, (to which Townsend does not provide an answer) how are these institutions and expectations of behaviour to be altered given the power and privileges of the top groups which he so impressively documents?

CONCLUSION

In trying to answer the apparently simple question, 'what is poverty?', one soon becomes aware that there are a number of competing definitions of poverty from which to choose. Which one chooses will affect one's conception of the extent of the problem, how one begins to explain its existence and the kind of policies one considers appropriate. Definitions range from the limited view which sees poverty solely in terms of survival, to wider views which relate poverty to the average standard of living and quality of life in a society and to its systems of production and distribution of resources. To see poverty as simply an insufficiency of basic needs may seem a neat solution, but it raises immediately the questions: 'what are basic needs' and 'how much satisfaction of needs would be considered to be "enough"?' Wider definitions face up to the fact of inequality in society and its causes and ask the question 'how much inequality is society prepared to tolerate?' The conclusion then is that radical change is needed to confront the problem of inequality. But correct as this may be in the long term it does not offer much solace to today's poor old-age pensioners, low-paid workers, long-term unemployed, or struggling single-parent families, who could be helped by short-term social reform.

Two major types of definition have been considered, the subsistence and the relative views of poverty. It is clear that even the subsistence or minimum definitions of poverty contain a relative component, for there are variations in what would be considered to be an acceptable minimum standard of living both within and between societies. While appearing precise and objective, in practice the act of drawing a poverty line always seems to involve the intrusion of subjective bias. Definitions which calculate factors in money-terms only are deficient in that they exclude those factors which are not easily reduced to cash terms, and omit criteria such as those seen by Townsend and Miliband to be crucial, especially *participation* and *power*.

Contained within the various definitions of poverty are explanations of its cause. From his surveys, Rowntree concluded that there were three stages in the life-cycle when poverty was most likely to occur: first, in childhood, then when one has children of one's own to support and rear, and finally when one is too old to work. Family needs vary at different stages of the life-cycle, and an income sufficient at one point would be insufficient at another. Many people run the risk of being poor at certain times in their lives. Other views see poverty as having more to do with exceptional circumstances, such as physical or mental illness or handicap, things which only the unfortunate few experience. The factors shown to be associated with poverty in numerous social surveys have not changed much since the nineteenth century, although the proportions of each category found among the poor and in the total population over time have varied. Obviously how far any of these may be viewed as 'exceptional circumstances' to be treated as the problem of a minority and dealt with by selective, specialised services is a question which underlies much of the discussion of poverty. It raises the questions of the causes of these conditions; how far they are inevitable; whose responsibility they are; and how far they reflect general features of society.

Chapter five

THE BATTLE OF IDEAS

The selectivist case was put clearly by Ian Macleod and Enoch Powell in 1952.

Given that redistribution is a characteristic of the social services, the general presumption must be that they will be rendered only on evidence of need, i.e. of financial inability to provide each particular service out of one's own or one's family's resources. Otherwise the process is a wasteful and purposeless collection and issue of resources, which leaves people in the enjoyment of the same facilities as before. (Macleod and Powell 1952: 5)

Enoch Powell made the same point when he stated

Upon this view the ascertainment of need is the essential preliminary to meeting need, though the ascertainment may take other forms than those which have given the term 'means test' its emotional and political content today. A means test and a pure social service go together. (*The Listener*, 17 April 1952)

Groups like the Conservative Political Centre and the Institute of Economic Affairs have pushed this view over the years. And Geoffrey Howe almost ten years later argued that 'over the whole field of social policy, the firm aim should be a reduction in the role of the State' (Howe 1961). Professor Alan Peacock, a leading Liberal economist, expressed the underlying philosophy when he said, 'the true object of the welfare state, for the Liberal, is to teach people to do without it' (Peacock 1961). Social services should not be viewed as permanent features of modern society, rather they should be regarded as crutches to be thrown away as soon as we learn to walk. Welfare should be returned to the private sector and where State services for the general population remain, the users should, as far as possible, meet the specific costs. State services for minorities with special needs should be restricted to those who cannot afford to provide for themselves in the private sector: that is, they should be offered according to means test. But this view rested on the optimistic assertion that the nation was becoming increasingly prosperous and that the problems with which the social services were initially intended to deal had largely been solved.

Advocates of the selectivist case see themselves as realistic men and they are critical of the impractical idealism of the universalists. They claim their approach to be a sensible response to the facts of welfare provision in contemporary Britain. The universalist principle has been applied and found wanting. Existing provision fails to meet real need adequately; institutions are preserved through inertia, although they are no longer either the most desired or efficient. Given the size of the total resources distributed, the limited outcomes of social provision (in alleviating poverty and meeting real needs) demonstrate the inefficiency of the system. To raise universal benefits, such as family allowances, to a level where they would have some impact on the problem would require a great increase in taxation with debilitating effects on economic life, reducing the incentive to effort and, consequently, the total size of the National Product. Such a policy would rebound on its supporters since the total resources available to meet the problem would be reduced not increased. To spend scarce resources administering a system which, in the majority of cases, takes money from the taxpayer with one hand and hands it back to him with the other is irresponsible. Far better to concentrate resources where they are really needed and where they can have the greatest effect.

The poor themselves do not share the fine sensibilities of their supposed allies. The reluctance to claim benefit is a characteristic only of the declining number of proud old people whose values and attitudes are not shared by the majority of claimants. The stigma associated with Poor Law provision and the harsh effects of the household means test of the 1930s have no meaning for those who have not experienced them. They are past history, no longer relevant. The problem now is rather one of too ready a willingness to rely on the system for support. This 'pocket-money' system encourages irresponsibility and lack of initiative. Furthermore, individual freedom is diminished where decisions about the allocation of resources are made by the State. A system allowing the exercise of individual preferences between services and benefits would direct resources more efficiently and with greater benefit since an individual's needs vary over time: constellations of needs are specific to each individual or household and therefore each man is the best judge of what he requires at any one time. Individual choice in the disposal of income directs resources in the most flexible and efficient way. In a selectivist system, inadequate or poor services would be subject to effective control. If they did not satisfy the demands of users, they would lose their financial support. Another result of State provision of welfare has been the growth of vast and complex bureaucracies, not subject to effective control, absorbing too high a proportion of skilled and talented manpower which is thereby lost to the industrial sector.

The selectivists argue for a streamlined system of State welfare provision which would ensure that benefits reach those who are in real need. The discipline of the market would reduce the number of malingerers and revive the values of individual responsibility, hard work, and reward for effort and talent. Taxation should be reduced and resources, including manpower, shifted from the public to the private sector. Welfare benefits should be subject to the regulation of the same economic forces that affect other commodities and be evaluated in comparison with these. Cash values would be the measure of standards, and individual choice regarding the disposal of cash would be the means to direct resources to needs. Absolute poverty is a residual problem in modern society and the needs of those in this condition should be met through the provision of selective services available after a test of means.

This view challenges the concept of collective responsibility for social welfare and emphasises instead the importance of individual responsibility. The social services should, in general, operate on the same economic principles as other goods available in the market and compete with them for resources. A reduced area of subsidised provision would remain for those clearly in need and too poor to meet the total cost of what they require. The emphasis is on providing cash benefits wherever possible rather than services in kind. The political philosophy of F.A. Hayek and the theories of the economist Milton Friedman lie behind and support these views. Both argue for a minimal role for the State and promote individualism and *laissez-faire* as preferable social and economic ideologies.

Milton Friedman has argued that Government measures do not help those they are supposed to help (BBC2 1 March 1980). Welfare programmes destroy independence. Those who are dependent on welfare are treated like children, trapped in the system within which a self-perpetuating cycle is set up. The actions of the State have deprived the poor of incentive. Their lives are dictated by rules. Job creation programmes and public housing schemes are unsuccessful and undermine moral fibre. More importantly, they encourage feelings of omnipotence in the bureaucrats who administer the schemes and feelings of dependency in those who receive them. They lead to fraud, waste and abuse. 'Government money always corrupts.' The best way to get anything done is to do it yourself. Individual effort and responsibility are preferable to patronage. Self-help by the poor themselves is the alternative. 'Trying to do good with other people's money simply has not worked.' (Friedman, 1980)

The universalists most certainly agree with many of these criticisms of the effects of a stigmatised and separate service for second-class citizens. They would agree that self-help, individual effort and responsibility are important virtues. The problem is what to do with those who cannot exercise self-help, who lack the necessary sterling qualities of physique and intelligence. Friedman plainly says that a combination of low-paid work and private charity is a preferable alternative to that of State provision. The poor, the sick and the weak would find a way to earn a living if they had to. His critics see this simple formula as a prescription for a society characterised by sweated labour, low wages, soup kitchens, dependence on charities, begging, street crime and the exploitation of the poor and weak – a return to nineteenth century conditions.

The aim of the universalists is to defend not to attack the Welfare State. However, they are severely critical of existing provision. A 'cradle to grave' system of adequate social security and social services has never been established and thus claims about its effects have no basis in fact. Universalistic principles are applied neither generally nor adequately. The aim of policy should be, therefore, the regeneration of the system, the extension of provision and a more thorough and committed application of the universalistic principle.

Universalism implies that whenever a person can be categorised as having needs which are officially recognised, for example, old age, unemployment and sickness, then an adequate income is paid as of right and without any test of other financial resources. This is an ideal to be aimed at for it exists hardly at all in the British system of social security. The insurance principle excludes residents or citizens who do not have the appropriate or adequate contribution qualifications, which are largely derived from participation in the paid labour force. Important sections of the community – women, the casually or seasonally employed, immigrants and school-leavers – have not been covered. In a universalistic system, access to social services would be available as of right to all citizens on equal terms. The application in practice of this principle has been less than hoped for: there are inequalities in access to services which reflect inequalities of information and ability to make use of the system, variations in provision between regions, cities and areas of a city, and differences in provision between sections of one service, certain needs being recognised while others are neglected.

The universalist case is that services should be dispensed in relation to need not to ability to pay. Since needs are various and complex, specialised services are required. The system should become more rather than less complex. However, some needs relate to circumstances and experiences which are likely to touch most people at some point in their lives, like childhood, old age, parenthood, becoming sick or unemployed. These experiences affect the majority of people, either themselves or their relatives and friends. The effect of such experiences on different income-groups is, however, quite different. Material resources, although never fully compensating, can cushion the effects of misfortunes like chronic sickness. Where there are inadequate material resources, severe deprivation will result. Without other resources, like family support, the situation deteriorates further. Public provision of welfare is able to prevent inequalities being reproduced and multiplied.

Some circumstances, like disability resulting from a traffic accident or cancer caused by working where exposed to asbestos, ought to be alleviated through public provision, since these circumstances are not necessarily the result of individual neglect or bad luck but the result of activities which the majority support and from which they benefit. The *disservices* of industrial society should be a communal responsibility. Meeting the needs of the unemployed ought similarly to be a collective responsibility since the level of employment is not amenable to individual control. The universalists argue for an extension of the categories for which public provision should be made and the recognition of collective responsibility, basing their argument on a moral code of duty to one's fellow citizens: misfortunes should be shared; fraternity and fellowship are the principles which should dictate policy. During the early 1950s, the universalists' case was influenced by the fact that, in conditions of rising material prosperity, social expenditure did not increase. The extension of social provision was clearly dependent not only on the quantity of available resources but also on the acceptance of the values of altruism, selflessness and equity. The harsher aspects of capitalism could be modified through social legislation if these values were accepted. There seemed less need then than in pre-war days to alter the economic system, which appeared to be delivering the goods and to be effectively regulated by the use of Keynesian techniques. The emphasis was more on persuading people to accept humane values.

To criticise the selectivist case, the universalists refer to the history of social administration. Wherever benefits and services have been distributed by income, one service has grown up for those able to pay and another for the poor. The latter service has invariably become a second-class service because resources are attracted to the higher status, better-endowed one. Differences in power reflect differences in material resources and these influence the type of service offered. Services for the poor are usually inferior and minimal. Having to use such services has involved loss of status and self-respect through association with a stigmatised section of the population, the submission to terms and methods of treatment which would not be accepted by other groups in society, such as the application of rules regarding private life and morals, inspection and scrutiny and a lack of opportunity to question the services provided. Once categorised as belonging to this second-class segment of society, integration into the rest of society becomes more difficult, as inferior and subordinate definitions and characteristics accumulate. Reorganisation along the lines suggested by the selectivists would be socially regressive. The universalists judge social progress in terms of the erosion of privilege, the establishment of social justice and the extension of political, civil and social rights to an increasing proportion of the population.

The universalists concede an admiration for the neat precision of the selectivist proposals but argue that they are simplistic and unworkable. The social, legal, political, cultural and psychological ramifications of an attempt to implement such policies would produce quite different consequences from those expected. These effects are equally as important as blind adherence to the principle of economic rationality and they would in practice prevent an efficient and beneficial allocation of resources. The basis of welfare provision should be an assessment of need. The test of the adequacy of a service lies in the extent to which it meets the complexity of defined needs. The universalists' criticism goes further than this, however – they do not underestimate their opponents' intelligence; they believe that the advocates of selectivism are aware of these ramifications and implications. The selectivist case was, they claim, intended as a deliberate attack upon the collectivist ethos. It was designed to have immediate popular appeal in offering reductions in taxation, cuts in the number of civil servants and the appearance of a bright, modern, streamlined service.

However, the universalists argue, the effect of such policies would be felt not just by the poor but by society as a whole. Separate services are socially divisive. Unintended consequences would be felt. The individual does not always have the ability to allocate resources in a way which is either to his own or society's benefit. Needs are not reducible to wants or choices between commodities. The individual lacks knowledge of specialised processes and is not always able to make the best choice between types of services available. With a shortage of resources, he is likely to emphasise immediate wants and simply 'hope for the best' regarding the future. Private provision would be based on actuarial principles: high risk categories would not be able to obtain the required services other than at very high cost, with the effect that the quality of life for some groups would be severely reduced, although the more fortunate would gain. The result of selectivist policies would be an increase in inequality. Wages would be reduced by throwing back on the wage-packet the costs of services now publicly provided. Competitive struggle would be established as the key principle of social life. Opportunities for profit-making through private provision of welfare would be extended, promoting the interests of pressure groups like the insurance companies, and the legal and medical professions. And, overall, the total amount spent on welfare services would be reduced through shifting patterns of expenditure towards the consumption of commodities produced in the private sector.

The 1950s saw a strong attack launched on the collectivist ethos. Many of the opinions and policies which had appeared extreme when first proposed by the selectivists had become accepted by as early as 1960. What remained of poverty in Britain was thought to be either eradicable through the natural processes of growth or a permanent residue of the irresponsible and unfortunate. Inequality was discussed less. But the universalists reopened the debate to demonstrate the continuance, not of isolated pockets of poverty, but of large numbers of people living in poverty or on its margins. And they tried to locate the source of poverty in the inequalities which have continued to operate in spite of social changes and reforms and which, they argue, have become more marked since the immediate post-war years. They emphasise the need for a continuing attack on inequalities in the distribution of resources. Established welfare provisions, which have redistributive effects, must be defended and pressure exerted to extend them. The universalistic principle should be applied in more areas of welfare provision. Private welfare, an important source of inequality, should be eliminated, particularly since it has detrimental effects on public provision. Those institutions and regulations which dehumanise the subject and diminish democratic rights should be attacked. The public must be informed about inequality and poverty.

Critics of this debate have taken issue with both sides. The most important counter-argument was clearly voiced by C.A.R. Crosland in *The Future of Socialism*, (1957), setting out the great *centrist* view shared by members of both parties until recent events undermined many of its assumptions. Crosland criticised the strict poverty approach of the selectivists on the grounds that it presents a gross and distorted account and would result in a worsening of conditions. Redistribution through the social services is not purposeless but involves a humane transfer of resources from the better-off to the worse-off, defined not in terms of income level, but from the healthy to the sick, from the young to the old, from the employed to the unemployed, from the single and childless to those with families. Such redistribution operates horizontally at every income level and does not require a test of means. Use of a means test would be unpopular and humiliating and would result in low take-up. The poor would be isolated as an underclass of dependents. Crosland's fundamental criticism of selectivism was that it accords too low a priority to social expenditure and would reduce it to a minimum. A similar argument, which had an important influence on Labour Party thinking, was that of J.K. Galbraith the American economist. In *The Affluent Society* (1958), he contrasted private affluence with public squalor and pointed to the need for increased State expenditure to improve the general quality of life. Society as a whole suffers where there is an over-emphasis on the conspicuous consumption of marketable commodities. Government action is needed to plan for society as a whole.

However, this centrist view also rejected the notion of 'free universality'. Crosland argued that this principle is not a necessary condition for social equality. He ridiculed the view as unrealistic and far-fetched: when one actually looks at the operation of the social services, 'it seems rather doubtful whether the fact that everyone now has an insurance card and repairs to the local post office, really does much to foster social equality' (Crosland 1963: 85). Universal subsistence benefits are neither sufficient for nor even particularly relevant to the promotion of social equality, which is more effectively promoted through an improvement in State services, especially in health, education and housing, leading to their being generally utilised by all sections of society. Private provision would lose its attraction as State services became comparable or superior. But general use of the same service does not require free access. Those who have the resources to meet the cost of such provision should do so – a means test would thus be an essential part of these State services. It would be however, a test of ability to pay not of the right of access to the service. For Crosland, poverty, welfare and equality were quite separate issues. The problem of poverty will always remain: rising material standards do nothing to reduce the area of need because standards of poverty change over time. But also, even were primary poverty to disappear, secondary poverty would remain, caused by a misuse of resources, irresponsible or ignorant spending habits. New needs would arise, particularly with the decline in family support, as a result of social and demographic changes, so that the need for a horizontal transfer of resources through time and between persons will continue. At every income level, families and old persons are badly off relative to single people and those in work, he argued. And those in distress caused by specific, unavoidable, individual misfortune will remain. Increasingly, selective provision will be required. The philosophy of the national minimum which underpinned the Beveridge proposals was to isolate broad categories, where needs could be presumed without individual investigation, and meet these by generous cash payments. The Beveridge objective was the elimination of want and want was assumed to be due to causes common to the entire population. This was the right approach at the time, said Crosland, but it must eventually give way to greater emphasis on selective services.

The difference between this 'centrist' proposal and that of the universalists is not in suggesting increased selective services – selectivity to reach special needs is accepted by both. Both also emphasise the need to increase social expenditure. The fundamental difference between them lies in their views of the causes of poverty. Crosland saw it as increasingly having to do with either misfortune or mis-spending, whereas the universalists' socialist view sees poverty as produced by the social and economic structure, as a class problem, not one of minority groups. Crosland's basic assumption, on which his arguments for an extension of social expenditure, refinement of categories and means of delivering services were based, was this: 'if our present rate of economic growth continues, material want and poverty and deprivation of essential goods will gradually cease to be a problem ... we shall increasingly need to focus attention, not on universal categories, but on individual persons and families: not on the economic causes of distress, but on social and psychological causes' (Crosland 1963: 96).

Basically, Crosland was working with an absolute definition of poverty, although accepting that the components might be more liberally defined over time. He did not accept the view that a markedly unequal share of resources leads to exclusion from social life or that poverty is the condition of those receiving the least resources in a system characterised by a maldistribution of income, wealth and other assets. He saw poverty as a residual problem and pointed to causes of poverty which universalists recognise but see as less widespread than material hardship. Arguing against Crosland, the universalists stress that material deprivation is the product of fundamental economic and political conditions which have not changed in post-war Britain. They argue that events have now proved his conception of the rate of economic growth to be overoptimistic. In placing economic growth as basic to the pursuit of socialist goals, Crosland paved the way for the priority attached to economic policy at the expense of social reforms, and they reject as naive his acceptance of private provision continuing in parallel with public provision. It was naive to expect the private sector to wither away and naive to underestimate the extent of opposition to continuing increases in social expenditure. This under-estimation of opposition resulted from viewing British society as one held together by consensus rather than as one divided by class conflict. It is this latter point which discriminates most clearly between the centrist and universalist arguments.

Recently, politics has become dominated by the failure to sustain high rates of economic growth and by Britain's declining position in world trade and international affairs. Argument has focused on how high a priority should be given to social policy in such circumstances, whether social expenditure has become a drain on the economy or whether it is a precondition for that social cooperation which is essential to economic survival. Rising unemployment and declining living standards point to issues some thought dead and buried: the debate on poverty and welfare has reverted to its earlier concern with the distribution of material resources between sections of society. Discussion of the needs of specially disadvantaged groups remains, however, together with other definitions of welfare, some of which (for example those criticising the detrimental effects of pollution and urban sprawl) attack the basic premise of the value of economic growth. How to finance social security and the social services remains the key question but answers differ radically, not simply on techniques of administration but also on the nature and feasibility of the 'good society'.

To summarise, the *centrist* position dominated in post-war years and can be located within the consensus politics of the post-war settlement. Those concerned to influence the policies of welfare and poverty tried to break through this consensus and shift the balance towards either the Left, the universalist position, or the Right, to selectivism. The centrist position was accepted by both Labour and Conservative Governments while 'Butskellism' ruled. In the 1970s, this consensus was shattered and the lines of debate were set between universalists, centrists and selectivists. With the election of the Thatcher Government of 1979, the selectivists made considerable gains. It remains to be seen whether this ideology can be put into practice and with what results.

These paradigms contain particular conceptions of poverty and the poor. In the years we are considering the view receded of the poor as part of the working class or as having interests shared in common by all citizens of the country. In its place came a conception of *pockets* of poverty, separate and distinct from the general affluence, to be explained by particular characteristics. Two paradigms which have especially influenced social administration in Britain see poverty as caused either by individual failure or by the special features of geographical areas, regions or the inner city. In both cases, the analysis concentrates on psychological and cultural issues and problems of social integration.

The view of poverty as residual, being confined to pockets of the unfortunate and irresponsible, and the distinction between the deserving and the undeserving poor, led to an emphasis on two distinct forms of treatment. The first involved specialised facilities catering to special needs. The second stressed the punishment and deterrence of rogues and malingerers. When particular cases are considered, however, opinion differs as to whether they are bad, mad or sad. Alcoholism, drug abuse and gambling, for example, contribute directly to the experience of poverty but they are forms of deviance which can be seen as either wilful irresponsibility, or as symptoms of a mental illness or personality disorder. In both views, individual inadequacy is emphasised rather than social conditions. The issue of 'scrounging on the State' falls clearly within this paradigm.

The selectivists have considered what factors predispose an individual to behave in ways likely to lead to poverty. Much attention has been given to the 'culture of poverty' and the 'cycle of deprivation', in which Sir Keith Joseph, as Secretary of State for Social Services in the early 1970s showed particular interest. These formulations emphasise the values, customs and attitudes associated with being poor and the way in which they prevent the children of the poor from moving out of the vicious circle of deprivation. The universalists rejected the emphasis placed on individual factors. In their view, structural patterns of inequality and injustice are basic to deprivation, fostering the conditions, social, economic and psychological in which the poor are trapped.

At a conference organised by the Pre-School Playgroups Association on 28 June 1972, Sir Keith Joseph discussed the *cycle of deprivation*. He posed the question 'why is it that in spite of long periods of full employment and relative prosperity and the improvement in community services since the Second World War, deprivation and problems of maladjustment so conspicuously persist?' He admitted that deprivation is an imprecise term. It may take many forms and show itself 'in poverty, in emotional impoverishment, in personality disorder, in poor educational attainment, in depression and despair'. By so linking these factors in one sentence, the emphasis was placed clearly on an explanation of poverty in terms of individual psychology. He went on, 'perhaps there is at work here a process apparent in many situations but imperfectly understood, by which problems reproduce themselves from generation to generation ... Social workers, teachers and others know only too well the sort of situation I am referring to, where they can be reasonably sure that a child, because of his background, is operating under disadvantage and prone to run into the same difficulties in his turn as his parents have experienced.' (Joseph 1972)

He called for more study of *transmitted deprivation*, a feature of those situations where standards have failed to rise. (This call led to the setting-up of a joint DHSS/SSRC study of transmitted deprivation.) Sir Keith Joseph made this notion a central plank of his policy proposals. His philosophy is one of individual responsibility and he has stressed the need to help individuals to function more adequately within society by better educational and social services for deprived families and better preparation for parenthood.

Peter Townsend described the *cycle of deprivation* as a confused thesis, 'a mixture of popular stereotypes and ill-developed, mostly contentious, scientific notions'. The central thesis was that 'inadequate people tend to be inadequate parents and that inadequate parents tend to rear inadequate children'. Supporting evidence came from studies of problem families, parental pathology and delinquency and inadequate mothering. Peter Townsend argued that this thesis: 'diverts our concern and our research endeavour from treating deprivation as a large-scale structural phenomenon to treating it as a residual personal or family phenomenon: it diverts us from considering potentially expensive to considering comparatively inexpensive policy measures; and it diverts us from ... blaming the Government to blaming ... the victim' (Townsend 1974).

The view of the poor as inadequate, lazy and as personal failures has a long history. The *incompetent poor* was an important category in the Elizabethan Poor Law. Later, concern shifted to *rogues and vagabonds* and the Vagrancy Laws which followed were concerned with discipline and punishment. This feature was also incorporated into the Poor Law Reforms of 1834. In recent years these two conceptions have also figured large: the cycle of deprivation concept emphasises the incompetent poor. The issue of *scroungers* refers to the category of *incorrigible rogues* and *those who will not work*. Attacks on the unemployed and the dole have claimed that large numbers of those claiming benefit are not unemployed at all but are part of the black or hidden economy, a view that has been propagated in certain newspapers. Concern with this issue led to the setting up of the Fisher Committee on the abuse of social security benefits, which reported in 1973. It showed that surveys by DHSS inspectors of more than 10,000 insured persons yielded fraud prosecutions of less than 1 per cent of claimants. Similarly low proportions have been found in other surveys.

These notions of the poor began to gain ground and were given legitimacy in the speeches of Ministers and politicians at the same time that similar views on immigrant groups were being aired. Both served to divide working people against themselves as they linked images of the poor with images of the immigrant. Policies for inner-city areas had the integration of immigrant communities and the control of racial tension very much in mind, although they were presented ostensibly as policies directed at the relief of poverty and inequality. Significantly, these policies were promoted not by the DHSS, but by the Home Office. Perceptions of the poor and of immigrant groups as distinctly different from other members of the working class are features of an ideological shift which both emanated from and fostered a reduction in working-class solidarity. American perspectives of a link between poverty and race and American paradigms of social policy and were absorbed and had considerable influence. This resulted intervention partly from the objective connection between race and the poverty of individuals and city areas but reflected also the dearth of ideas in British social administration. And it represented a significant ideological shift towards individualistic rather than class values.

The conception of poverty as an urban problem led to a shift in policy in the mid-1960s towards the funding of more regional and area projects. These programmes aimed to alleviate urban poverty, educational deprivation, inner-city decline, urban disorder and regional underdevelopment. Educational priority areas were defined. Urban programmes included Urban Aid, the Community Development Projects and partnerships between local and central government. The emphasis of these projects was on intervention to deal with the structural roots of poverty and with the social control and integration of those affected.

Ideas of poverty as rooted in personal inadequacy or in the special problems of urban areas led to policy initiatives which departed from the traditional concern of social security provision with the redistribution of income and cash benefits to individuals suffering from defined social hazards. These policies reflected a greater concern with social integration and problems of law and order. The idea was to prevent poverty by intervening in the socialisation process in the home, school or neighbourhood. The perceptions of poverty and the policies which followed marked off the poor as a distinct social category. It will not be surprising, therefore, to find these attitudes reflected in public opinion. A recent survey carried out in the member countries of the European Community on *The*

Perception of Poverty in Europe provides fascinating evidence of the rightward shift in attitudes in Britain and the distinctively harsh views of the British compared to people in other European countries (Commission of the European Communities 1977).

In the UK, only 8 per cent said that they often saw people who were in poverty. Twenty-eight per cent thought there were people who were poor but they never saw them, and 64 per cent thought there were no poor people. Those who believed there were still people living in poverty were asked why this was so. Fifty-three per cent thought the poor had always been poor, that is, were a distinct social category. The three most common causes of poverty given by these UK respondents were, heading the list, *laziness* (45%), followed by *chronic unemployment* (43%) and *drink* (40%). *Laziness*, which was the most commonly stated reason in the UK, came fifth in the table when answers from respondents in the whole Community were pooled. (Only 28 per cent of all European answers referred to this.) Only 11 per cent thought *laziness* a reason for poverty in the Netherlands, 15 per cent in France, 29 per cent in Italy and 30 per cent in Germany. Similarly *drink*, mentioned by 40 per cent of the British, was the answer of 28 per cent of the Community respondents as a whole. The three most common causes of poverty mentioned in the whole community were *deprived childhood, lack of education* and *sickness or ill-health*, all features outside individual control. Only chronic unemployment could be seen as such of the answers favoured by the British, while laziness and drink clearly refer to individual inadequacy. Similarly distinct differences appeared in answers to the question, 'why are there people who live in need?' Four opinions were offered from which respondents had to choose the one which corresponded most closely with their own: 1. because they have been unlucky; 2. because of laziness and lack of will power; 3. because there is much injustice in our society; 4. it's an inevitable part of modern progress. In Italy and France, the most common response was to accuse society. In the UK, the tendency was to accuse the victim. A startling 43 per cent of UK answers cited *laziness and lack of will – power* as the reason. This was twice that of other European respondents (25% of Community respondents overall gave this answer). In all countries it was found that the poorer income groups, the less well educated and the non-leaders tended to blame the victims. Fifty-three per cent of the British thought there was less poverty today than ten years ago. Sixty-two per cent thought that the poor had a chance of escaping from poverty and 73 per cent that their children had such a chance.

Only 7 per cent of respondents in the EEC countries as a whole thought the authorities do too much to combat poverty: in the UK, 20 per cent gave this opinion. Only 36 per cent of UK respondents thought the authorities do too little; 54 per cent of all respondents in the Community as a whole gave this answer.

The survey went on to draw up a typology of attitudes to poverty and divided respondents into groups. Three types tended to perceive poverty as existing in their society but had different attitudes towards policy: the 'militants for justice' (10%), a young, educated, activist minority, which tended to contest the society in which they lived; the 'optimists' (11%), a more moderate and less committed group, preferring reform to revolution; and the 'passive type' (13%) from whom little could be expected in the way of political involvement. Others scarcely or never perceived poverty: these were the 'cynics' (14%), the 'non-malicious egoists' (6%), the 'well-informed/well-intentioned' (39%) and the 'pessimists' (7%) (those who were unwilling or too despairing to act). The relative importance of these different types in the different countries is very revealing. The most common category in the UK was that of the 'well-intentioned' (37%), as it was in the EEC as a whole. These are the nice, comfortable people of the suburbs whose attitudes are generally benign but who do not consider poverty to be a problem. However, the next most important category in the UK was that of the 'cynics' (27%). This represents a far larger proportion than in any other EEC country. (The country in which the category occurred next most frequently was Germany, with 17% being placed in that type. Other countries had between 7% and 13% of respondents in this group.) The survey describes the 'cynics' as 'quite incontestably ... the hard core of social egoism and conservatism of the most reactionary type. "Poverty? What's that?" This type is particularly common in the UK, which seems to suggest that it is tied up with a set of beliefs whereby the poor are primarily responsible for their social disgrace.' (Commission of the European Communities 1977: 83)

In the light of these findings and the clear swing to the right in the 1979 election, the future of the poor in Britain seems bleak indeed. However, there are constraints other than ideology acting on government policy: some we have considered in earlier chapters – social structure, population changes and changes in social and public institutions. Others are political factors, and the influence of pressure groups, both inside and outside government services. It is to these political influences that we now turn.

Chapter six
THE SUBORDINATION OF THE POOR

The failure to confront the persisting problems of poverty and insecurity in British society is the direct result of the political system which prevailed in post-war years. These political arrangements are the key to understanding why the poor continued to be neglected, why the problem remained in spite of reliable information, clear policy proposals and an affluent society. The political will for reform was weak. This has been depicted as a moral problem, reflecting the growth of cynicism, selfishness and materialism and the dominance of hostile attitudes towards the poor. These developments were fortified by the pursuit of stability and 'consensus politics'.

The year 1945 marked the point at which the electorate gave the Labour Party, for the first time, an overall parliamentary majority, validating in public the claim to be the natural alternative to the Conservatives which had already been substantiated in 1940. So began a period of twenty years when nearly all the deep objectives of the state – and of most governments since the mid-1920s – in economic planning, social welfare, harmony and the avoidance of crisis seemed to have been achieved. (Middlemas 1979: 371)

The Labour Party rode to power on a wave of popular radicalism in 1945 and established through legislation the institutions we call the Welfare State. Gradually in the years that followed popular radicalism waned, the Conservative Party came to accept the Welfare State and the Labour Party lost the drive to reform. The Labour movement suffered a crisis of identity, but emerged reintegrated as a party of social democracy. Consensus politics reflected the acceptance of the Welfare State by the Conservatives and the dominance of social democracy in the Labour movement, in a period which saw a dilution in the strength of class-consciousness, especially

where it informed voting behaviour. In a system of two-party electoral competition, the trend to the centre was encouraged by the
constant search for the middle ground. This system began to break
down in the late 1960s and reached its nadir in 1974, when the
collapse of the two-party system appeared to produce a collapse of
government. Disillusion with established politics and with the
major parties symbolised the rejection of previous political agree-
ments and the death of consensus politics. With this breakdown in
the older form of achieving political stability, polarisation of the
parties grew, although the divisions within each were as strong as
the divisions between them.

The most interesting aspect of the development of consensus
politics is that it emerged from the adoption of welfare and
economic management schemes incompatible with either socialist
or free – market ideas. The main institutions of the Welfare State
rested on the essentially Liberal ideas of Beveridge, Keynes and
Rowntree reflecting the common ground between Liberal Radicalism and Labourism. These plans centred importantly on the idea of
a supposedly neutral government – an idea quite at odds with concepts of class or sectional interest. It was precisely the failure of this
system to deal with conflicts of class and sectional interest that led
to its collapse. It had survived longer than it might have been
expected to do largely because of the historically unique period of
rapidly rising living standards which followed the Second World
War. Inflation, recession and unemployment posed problems for
the system which it was unable to solve and led to its inevitable
demise.

To maintain the appearance of consensus and political stability
in the face of conflict and antagonism required a careful balancing
of political forces and an accommodation to the strength of certain
sections at the expense of others. The effect was also to alter fund-
amentally the nature of the political system and especially to shift
the locus of power from the traditional system of parties and Parliament and extend it to a wider range of institutions which grew
up with the Welfare State and, importantly, incorporated representatives of the trade unions and employers' federations. The rise of
what Middlemas calls 'governing institutions' – more than
pressure-groups but not at the centre of state authority – mediating
between their mass membership and government, is the crucial
feature of this system of political arrangements. (Governing institutions are 'bodies which have been recognised by government as
bargaining partners, granted permanent rights of access and

accorded devolved powers by the state' (Middlemas 1979: 381).)
The politics of institutional collaboration marks the character of
this political formation. The system avoided, by compromise,
'crises in sensitive areas like wages and conditions, public order,
immigration, unemployment, or the position of women . . . by the
alternate gratification and cancelling out of the desires of large,
well-organised, collective groups to the detriment of individuals,
minorities and deviants' (Middlemas 1979: 18).

It is this feature of the poor's exclusion from power along with
other deprived groups, which explains the neglect of this issue in
British political life. The powerlessness of the poor has of course
been referred to by others to explain their continuing miserable
plight. But it has more often been seen as yet one more characteristic of those individuals who are poor, which, added to their age,
sickness, isolation, lack of education or what have you, is sufficient
to explain their social condition. The powerlessness of the poor
does not, however, follow necessarily from their individual characteristics but is produced by a political system which specifically
excludes them from the exercise of decision-making: a political system, that is, which represents an alliance of certain interests at the
expense of others.

It is important to understand how this political system has worked if we are to explain how the poor came to be neglected. Both political parties contain within them currents of ideas which recognise a
responsibility towards the poor. Within the Conservative Party the
ideas of Tory paternalism and concern for political stability support
the interests of the poor. Within the Labour Party, ideas of social
justice, fellowship and compassion recognise the claims of social
reform. The neglect of the poor has then to do with the varying
fortunes of these forces within the parties as well as with the relative strength of parties and Parliament within the overall system of
power. The ascendancy of the 'free-marketeers' in the Conservative
Party and the inadequacy and consequent defeat of social democracy in the Labour Party are part of this account. The concentration on economic management to the neglect of social policy by all
parties to the tri-partite system of government is the other part.
Political forces have proved weak compared to the other elements
involved in the system of tri-partite corporate management.

In a system of consensus politics, with its ideology of neutral
government and the national interest there is a strong tendency for
parties, pressure-groups and interest-groups and, particularly, political theories and concepts to lose ground to the forces of the State,

capital and labour. Politics is reduced to a competition between political elites occurring in stylised fashion once every few years and acted out largely under the direction of public relations experts and aimed at the middle ground. Such a system is manifestly incapable of resolving fundamental disputes and conflicts and it broke down during the years 1967 to 1976. What will replace it is not yet clear. The present political instability and open conflict may be resolved by a move to a more authoritarian State or to one which allows greater recognition of trade union power and influence. In either circumstance the problem of the dispossessed will remain, but it is clearly a problem which would be dealt with quite differently under each system. The resolution of the present crisis of political instability will outweigh the problem of the poor in the short term, while to continue to neglect them will only store up problems for the future. An analysis of the ways in which the poor have been excluded from politics will inform our thinking about strategies for the short-term so as to bind them into a coherent plan of action for a political system which includes within it the participation of the poor.

After the Second World War, Governments assumed responsibility for economic management using Keynesian methods rather than physical planning and controls. There was not much enthusiasm for the retention of controls within either Government or the Labour movement and this, combined with the opposition of bankers, bureaucrats and the United States, was sufficient to ensure that it was never seriously debated. Because of the lack of planning and of an acceptable incomes policy, post-war Governments have continuously had to react to balance-of-payments or inflation crises rather than pursue viable policies of economic management, so it is not only the concentration on economic policy to the neglect of social policy, but the dominance of a particular kind of economic problem, that of crisis, which lies at the root of the matter.

Provision has been made for a National Health Service in England and Wales; for the creation of a national scheme of insurance against industrial injuries in place of the present system of workmen's compensation and for the expansion and improvement of the existing schemes of social insurance. A system of family allowances and the higher rates of old age pensions under the new social insurance scheme have been brought into operation. (Prorogation, King's Speech, 6 December 1946)

Acts have been passed to abolish the Poor Law and establish arrangements for assistance to all in need, and to make improved provision for children deprived of a normal home life. Thus has been discharged the great task, which it has fallen to this Parliament to undertake, of giving legislative effect to a comprehensive scheme of social security. That scheme, which has now been brought into operation, will promote the health and well-being of My People, provide a substantial resource in any periods of unavoidable unemployment and relieve those anxieties which in the past so often attended sickness, disability or old age. (Prorogation, King's Speech, 13 September 1948)

Having discharged this great task, had the Labour Party lost its major good cause? Was there nothing left to reform?

Historically, the Labour Party had a greater concern for domestic issues whereas the Conservatives were more interested and effective in foreign affairs. The Labour Party had promoted the issues of comprehensive social security, a free universal health service and the maintenance of full employment since at least the 1920s. Social policy then had shared an equal place with industrial and financial reorganisation in Labour's programmes and was seen as integrally linked with these plans. Once these were accepted, the campaigns of the Labour Party seemed to be rendered obsolete. Labour lost the initiative and has developed few new ideas in social policy since the 1940s, for, to some extent, Labour has shared the general complacency that poverty was disappearing. Even where concern has grown, with awareness of the continuance of poverty, Labour's reaction has been generally defensive, defending the institutions which were established in the 1940s and arguing that all would be well if only more money were pumped into them. The main priority within the party, after the failure of 'social justice' to appeal to the electorate as a campaign issue in 1959, has been to become recognised as a national party, capable of managing the economy more successfully than the Conservatives.

Labour attained power in 1945 largely because of the experiences of the 1930s and memories of the disillusionment that followed the First World War. Public pressure to implement the Beveridge Report and establish a national health service was strong and Labour was recognised to be the party most likely to succeed in this. The party therefore had an interest in proclaiming the success of the 'Welfare State', but was less ready to recognise any defects. 'Labour has honoured the pledge it made in 1945 to make social security the birthright of every citizen. Today destitution has been banished', said the Party Manifesto in 1950. The Party presented itself as the guardian of the Welfare State, the party which could be trusted to protect the interests of the sick, the poor and the old.

The Conservatives were portrayed as mean, and likely to make drastic cuts in the services. The theme of the campaign was compassion, cooperation and citizenship. Universalism – the principle which forged the alliance of the middle class and organised labour – was emphasised: social legislation was to the benefit of the whole community. The emphasis on social justice continued in the 1951 campaign, but no new policies were proposed. The concern was to protect what had been created against Tory attack, and the spectre of conditions in the inter-war years was raised to support this threat:

Then millions suffered from insecurity and want. Now we have social security for every man, woman and child. Then we had the workhouse and the Poor Law for old people. Now we have a national insurance system covering the whole population with greatly improved pensions and a humane National Assistance scheme. (Labour Manifesto 1951)

The Tories 'would take us backward into poverty and insecurity at home and grave perils abroad'.

The Labour leadership was, however, tired and exhausted of ideas. They thankfully gave up the fight and handed over government to the incoming Conservative administration. The old leadership of Attlee, Bevin, Morrison, Dalton, Cripps was in decline. The defeat of 1951 led to recrimination and strife and the following years were bleak indeed for the Labour Party, dominated by the battle between Aneurin Bevan and Herbert Morrison to succeed Attlee and by doubts and confusion whether to go for more socialism (meaning mainly nationalisation) or to consolidate and improve the great post-war gains. What did the voters want? Electoral considerations could not be separated from discussions of policy.

The 1955 campaign ran on similar lines to that of 1951. The Labour Party claimed responsibility for the establishment of the social services in the 1940s and again contrasted this with the earlier days: 'Through the National Health Service and National Insurance, the Labour Government began to abolish the fear of old age, sickness and disablement which haunted working class life before the war.' (Labour Manifesto 1955) Early in the 1950s, concern began to be voiced for those groups who were not sharing the fruits of the consumer society. There was growing evidence of the plight of the poor, especially of those on national assistance. Labour reluctantly recognised the continuing problems of discrimination and stigma associated with poverty and referred to the need to remove 'the last taint of public assistance'. The creation of a Ministry of Social Welfare was proposed which would take over the work not only of the Ministry of Pensions and National Insurance, but also of the National Assistance Board. The impact of inflation on fixed incomes was recognised and Labour proposed an annual review of benefits, pensions and allowances to link them with rises in the cost of living.

What was to become the central question for social policy in the next two decades arises in Labour's manifesto of 1955:

We welcome the growth of superannuation schemes in industry and commerce as valuable additions to National Insurance pensions. We shall consult with the TUC and industry with a view to extending similar schemes on a voluntary basis to all kinds of employment and will seek wherever possible to arrange for pensions to be made transferable.

Clearly Labour had accepted the continued existence of private welfare and that national insurance would provide only a floor below which no-one should fall. Rising above this level would be the result either of individual effort and private insurance or of the fruits of collective bargaining by unions on behalf of their members. Those unable to afford private insurance, those not acceptable to private insurance schemes and those in non-unionised or weakly-organised occupations and/or working for non-progressive employers would have to rely on the basic minimum. The distinction between the dependent and low-paid poor on the one hand and organised labour on the other, implanted in the legislation of the 1940s, was thus nourished. Twenty years later it came to fruition in an anti–welfare backlash.

The regeneration of the Labour Party began after the leadership settled on Hugh Gaitskell in December 1955. He was to be leader for seven years until his untimely death. His rival Bevan coined the label which stuck: Gaitskell was a 'dessicated calculating machine', whose accession seemed to symbolise the transformation from socialism to social democracy as one from emotion and fire to cold reason. The promotion of working-class grievances gave way to the protection of the Welfare State and the mixed economy. Such 'revisionism' has sometimes been equated with consensus politics and the ideology of the managed economy. It was the distinctive feature of the social democracy of this period in the Labour Party, the badge of the new Labour intellectuals, but it was one which seemed to run counter to the sound instincts of the Labour voter, who John Saville commented, was better aware of the appalling housing conditions that remained and the fact that for many industrial workers a decent family income was only possible if the wife of the family also worked: 'The commonsense scepticism of the working-class was abundantly justified. The facts of life did not square with all the talk of massive social changes, and the inflated claims made by Labour publicists only increased the general disbelief.' (Saville 1965: 157)

It was, however, only later in the 1960s that traditional supporters were neglected in favour of winning the votes of the new white-collar technocrats. Gaitskell was passionate in his commitment to social democracy. He and his circle retained faith in fellowship, social justice and personal freedom: social justice in no way inspired with class hatred was fundamental. They had great faith in the power of reason both to find the answers to social problems and to persuade men to 'see the light'.

It was Gaitskell's leadership which gave Richard Crossman the opportunity to develop and present social policy. In 1957, Crossman announced, to loud acclaim from the Annual Conference at Brighton, Labour's *National Superannuation Plan*, which aimed to provide the benefits of superannuation to all contributors to national insurance. The Plan was to some extent redistributive and had been meticulously worked out by the combined labour of that trio of experts in social administration, Richard Titmuss, Peter Townsend and Brian Abel-Smith, aided by Crossman himself, who would eventually be responsible for providing renewed impetus to Labour's plans for a pensions policy in the late 1960s.

This plan for national superannuation formed a central plank in Labour's campaign for social reform in the late 1950s. By this time, 'revisionism' or the social democratic view had become the dominant strain in Labour thinking. A concern for social reform did not imply a radical upheaval in the organisation of society. The movement for social reform was to be fuelled by the economic growth which would result from the application of Keynesian methods of managing the mixed economy. Roy Jenkins argued in 1959 that Labour's main domestic policies would aim at economic expansion at home, but that these policies would provide a more just, as well as a more prosperous society (Jenkins 1959). However, in addition, tough-sounding references to 'technical skill', 'economic policies geared towards increased material prosperity' and 'realism' began to be emphasised to combat the view of Labour as the party of woolly, idealistic, tender-minded socialists.

Labour's 1959 election campaign concentrated on the issue of social reform, giving prominence to those left behind by acquisitive consumerism, a theme owing much to Galbraith's discussion of the contrast between private affluence and public squalor in his book, *The Affluent Society*. The argument was offered that the public services had been starved of funds in the 1950s, partly, it was implied, as a deliberate attempt to neglect them and diminish their quality, to prove the case that private enterprise worked better, and partly the result of the selfishness and meanness of Tories. It was certainly the case that public expenditure not only did not rise but actually fell in most years of the 1950s. The second-class quality of the social services used by working people contrasted with the superior quality of either private welfare schemes and fringe benefits or those sections of the public services used extensively by the middle classes. In the competition between public and private services, the public sector was being unfairly held back, partly through the use of wage regulation in the public sector to hold down the overall income level. The inadequacies and scandalous conditions existing in many areas of the social services were documented impressively in essays in the volume *Conviction*, particularly influential being those by Peter Townsend and Brian Abel-Smith (MacKenzie 1958).

The dominant theme was that put forward by Crosland, the importance of the promotion of greater social equality through the reform of the educational system, re-distribution of the tax structure and an increase in the proportion of the national income spent by the Government on social welfare. With a continually rising revenue available to government, the public services would steadily improve and, in the competition with private services, come to be seen as clearly superior, so that it would be unnecessary to attempt a takeover of these private services. They would wither away in the radiance from the improved public sector.

The Labour Party in its 1959 election manifesto focused on the problems of those who had lost out in the race for prosperity, widowed mothers, the chronic sick, the 400,000 unemployed and the millions of old-age pensioners who had no adequate superannuation. This problem of the 'submerged fifth' was the 'greatest social challenge of our time'. Labour contrasted the 'haves' with the 'have nots', and conducted a campaign on behalf of the 'have nots'. At the same time, they stressed their commitment to demand-management, a device which, it was thought, would expand production. The prosperity that would follow would then be fairly shared.

Labour's plan for national superannuation was given prominence. It would offer to all the advantages of the best kind of private scheme and, when in full operation, would provide half-pay on retirement for the average wage-earner. In addition, old-age pensions and widow's pensions would be increased. The 'national disgrace' of the poverty of half the old-age pensioners in Britain would be remedied.

Labour appealed to the working population as a whole with its offer of national superannuation and to the altruism of the voters. Its social policies were designed to improve the relative position of the 'have-nots', the vulnerable, dependent population. Their alternative financial policies, based on Keynesian economics, would provide the key to success. The electorate found this difficult to accept, particularly since, in general, the economic policies of the Conservatives seemed to be quite effective in producing the material prosperity which contrasted with pre-war days and the days of austerity of the last Labour Government.

In 1959, therefore, the poor and the deprived still had a voice in political affairs through the medium of the Labour Party. But the crucial weakness in Labour's campaign was its insistence that these social benefits could be delivered without increasing taxation. The public, quite sensibly, had its doubts. The assertion that improved social services would not cost more confirmed the stereotype of fanciful, socialist idealists, whose policies were imbued with laudable good intentions but were quite impracticable. 'Tory propagandists allege that a Labour Government would have to put up taxes in order to pay for these improved social services. This is quite untrue.' (Labour Party Manifesto 1959) The promises seemed even more doubtful when the Labour Party claimed that not only would it be able to improve welfare without increasing taxation but that the increased revenue derived from economic expansion (which would result from the application of its budgetary and other policies) would actually allow it to reduce taxation and repay post-war credits. 'The steadily expanding national income will enable us to pay for our five-year programme without increasing the rates of taxation.' Some of this would also be paid for by an attack on tax-dodgers and tax-free benefits. But the careful British public was not taken in by these 'pie-in-the-sky' promises.

The Labour Party would not have made this mistake if it had made a correct assessment of social and economic trends. Underlying all their statements is the clear assumption that the social reforms required to remedy the 'national disgrace' would not cost very much to implement. Severe and scandalous as was the plight of the dependent population, the problem was seen as confined to a relatively small section. On the whole, the Welfare State was working well but there were areas which needed special attention. The problem of continually rising social expenditure under the pressure of demographic, technical and social changes was not foreseen. The over-estimation of future rates of economic growth, which has bedevilled the planning of future public expenditure since, was present in Labour statements at this election.

On the whole poverty was thought to have been abolished. 'Modest prosperity' described the situation of most working people. Policies directed at the alleviation of poverty were no longer the direct concern of the majority of Labour voters. Plans for social security for the working population as a whole did not embrace the special needs of the dependent population for which separate plans were required. The explicit recognition of a split in social policy between strategies for social security and plans for assistance for the poor and needy was not, of course, a new perspective. The institutions of the Welfare State of the 1940s recognised this division with the split between national insurance and national assistance. What was different, however, was the growing acceptance that poverty could not be prevented. Apart from those who denied that poverty did exist in the late 1950s, who were few in the Labour Party, most had to explain why this was the case. Rather than look critically at the operation of the Welfare State, still in many ways a flower in the cap of the Labour Party, the explanation of poverty adopted was that of individual or family circumstances, inadequacy and unemployability.

The two main currents in Labour thinking at this time come together in a quotation from Roy Jenkins' *The Labour Case* (1959). Accepting Peter Townsend's calculation that a fifth of the population had not shared in the general improvement in living standards, an improvement brought about more by full employment than better social services, he remarks:

Any believer in social justice, or indeed any believer in a civilised society, must surely give a high priority to providing such an improvement. Some, including Mr Townsend himself, would give it an absolute priority. They would deny the right of those whose standard of living is already at or above the average to any further improvement until the submerged fifth had been given more or less equivalent benefits. I would not accept this extreme position. Neither the economic policy of a nation nor the political programme of a party is likely to achieve a successful dynamism if it is based solely upon the assistance of lame ducks. (Jenkins 1959: 56–7)

Thus advocacy of equality was cast as extremism. The need for incentives was accepted if economic growth were to be attained; and any chance of winning an election on proposals for social justice was 'realistically' denied.

The change in Labour thinking during the 1950s is clearly summed up there. The notion of social justice integral to ethical socialism, which had been absorbed into the social democracy of Gaitskell and his circle, was relegated to a rhetorical niche and replaced by realism and pragmatism. With Gaitskell's death the inspiration went out of Labour politics to be replaced by a cynicism which passed for realism.

The proposals for social justice made at this time may indeed have been naive, underestimating as they did the extent of the problem and thus the resistance to paying for the services. The poor's voice in political affairs was heard and was rejected by the electorate. Now the poor were a minority, elections would not be fought on the claims of the poor, although pressure groups might try to bring these issues to bear on the consciences of Ministers.

With the loss of its third successive election, the Labour Party entered a period of soul-searching, emerged as a strong alternative to the Conservatives and came to dominate the political scene for the next decade and a half. But pragmatism and realism were to be the order of the day, and little or no real priority was given to 'social justice' or ethical and moral questions. The Christian and humanitarian ethics of British socialism, an integral part of the writings of Tawney, for example, whose book *Equality*, first published in 1931, was the bible of earlier socialists, were displaced from the Labour Party to reappear in pressure groups devoted explicitly to advocating the interests of the powerless poor and deprived. The causes which had been promoted by Labour in the first half of the century gave way to the desire to be recognised as the natural party of government. The initiative for social reform passed from the political party to extra-parliamentary groups.

It was not that these causes were no longer seen as 'good'. But they were no longer the concern of the majority of Labour supporters, rather they were the problems of various minorities best served by pressure groups. The Labour Party was responding to what it saw as a change in its social base. It had never been a party of ideology, in spite of its rhetoric and singing of 'The Red Flag' at Party conferences. It has been from its inception primarily a party of interest and the main interests represented are those of the trade unions and the working man.

According to a survey conducted in 1959 for a Penguin Special, *Must Labour Lose*, the image held of the Party by its own supporters could be indicated by five commonly held statements: 'it stands mainly for the working class; it is out to help the underdog; it would extend the welfare services; it is out to raise the standard of living of ordinary people; and it would try to abolish class differences' (Abrams and Rose 1960). The authors commented that this image of the Labour Party held by its own supporters was unlikely to lead to a more successful future. Their conclusion was that the Labour Party should give greater emphasis to its ability to improve domestic material prosperity if it hoped to win the next election. This would be more appealing to the electorate than its present image as 'the party of poor people, old-age pensioners, factory workers and people interested in helping the underdog' (Abrams and Rose 1960: 20). Labour should try to capture from the Conservatives 'ambitious people, middle-class people, young people, office workers and scientists. All these types are expanding in number today and are likely to go on expanding.' (op. cit.: 21)

The image of the Labour Party held by both its supporters and non-supporters is one which is increasingly obsolete in terms of contemporary Britain. Both groups see Labour as identified with the working class – *especially the poor and the labouring working class*; and at the same time, many workers irrespective of their politics no longer regard themselves as working class. Conversely the electorate sees the Conservative Party as the party of middle-class people and young people, the party that attracts men and women with realistic ideals and which offers prosperity to all and opportunities to the ambitious. (idem.: 23 – my italics)

It was accepted that the working-class ethos of solidarity and mutual help had been eroded by social mobility and prosperity. The increasing strength of the trade unions allowed workers to improve their situation through collective bargaining without the support of the Parliamentary Party. The Parliamentary Party should retain a special interest in the 'casualties of the Welfare State' and other minority groups and put into practice its 'socialist idealism' in protecting these groups. The party in Government should also stand for the improvement and protection of communal interests and social needs which could not be served by the pursuit of individual and sectional interests. (It was not recognised that a conflict might arise between the purposes of the two wings of the Party). The Party's electoral appeal to the middle ground was founded on its claim to manage the economy more successfully than its opponents, partly because of its Keynesian policies and technical competence (Wilson the economist with his computers rather than Douglas-Home the aristocrat and his match-sticks) but mainly because of its understanding with the trade unions.

In 1964 Labour, now led by Harold Wilson, presented itself at the polls, however, not as having lost its concern with social justice but simply as having changed the emphasis. Its first task would be, as in 1959, the creation of new wealth – but this time it was more convincing about its ability to do so. And having attained economic growth, a sufficient part of the new wealth created would go to meet 'urgent and now neglected human needs'. Provision for social casualties and communal needs would have to await the creation of new wealth, apart from immediate measures to alleviate these conditions, but all were optimistic that this could be achieved. Labour's interest in 'social policy' was, however, now distinct from 'social justice'. A new direction to social security was foreseen, tying it in closely with the demands of manpower planning. The Plan for Industry involved 'security and mobility': the right to compensation for loss of job or disturbance; the right to half-pay maintenance during any period of sickness or unemployment; rights to industrial training and retraining; and full transferability of pension entitlements. The winning of the trade unions' cooperation in economic management relied heavily on these proposals for phasing and cushioning the effects of change.

In 1963 a sample of voters was asked what they thought were the most important problems facing the Government. Welfare issues were commonly mentioned in the replies, especially pensions, the welfare of old people, and the health service. Family allowances were singled out for unfavourable comment. In the early 1960s, public opinion favoured increased government spending on pensions and housing. Those who favoured expansion in the social services saw Labour as the party most likely to carry this through. In the election of 1964, a sample of voters was asked, 'which party would be more likely to spend more on social services?': 69 per cent thought Labour more likely to do so, 16 per cent thought there was not much difference between the parties and 8 per cent answered 'Conservative', (7 per cent did not know).

Labour had conducted a vigorous campaign in the early sixties to demonstrate the existence of poverty, particularly among old-age pensioners. Thus its plans for the improvement of the social services and social security were given some prominence and, since public opinion favoured reform, the promise to spend more on the social services acted to its advantage. Labour also recognised the inter-relationship of the tax and social security systems and promised a major overhaul of both.

Labour's social policies at this time reflect two of the main pressures on government in a period of consensus politics and institutional collaboration: the need to concede to trade union interests and the need to react to public opinion to win the electoral competition. Advocacy of a relative definition of poverty led to the proposal that national insurance benefits would be raised initially and thereafter linked to average earnings (not rises in the cost of living) 'so that as earnings rise so too will benefits'. But the major new proposal was for a 'wage-related scheme', the aim of which would be half-pay benefits for the worker on average pay. This scheme obviously figured large in Labour's plans, for it was implemented relatively quickly. Its plans for national superannuation, however, did not come before Parliament until 1970, and lost out in the change of Government. The promise of an incomes guarantee, laying down a new national minimum benefit for the retired and for widows, did not materialise at all. The priority given to the earnings-related schemes for sickness and unemployment reflects their connection with industrial policy and manpower planning. 'In a period of rapid industrial change it is only elementary justice to compensate employees who, through no fault of their own, find that their job has disappeared', Labour's manifesto stated. The other advantage of these schemes, over those for pensions and an incomes guarantee for other National Assistance recipients, was that they would make relatively little demand on the Exchequer and would not involve more radical policies of redistribution.

Labour recognises that the nation cannot have first-rate social security on the cheap. That is why we insist that the new wage-related benefits must be self-supporting and must be financed in the main by graded contributions from employers and employees. For the same reason we stress again, that, with the exception of the early introduction of the Income Guarantee, the key factor in determining the speed at which new and better levels of benefit can be introduced will be the rate at which the British economy can advance. (Labour election manifesto 1964)

Not all members of the Labour Party avoided the issue of redistribution, however. In 1960, Rita Hinden had concluded:

... the big battle now before us is concerned with the division between private and public spending. On the one hand lie the claims of the private citizen to acquire personal possessions, to live in a comfortable home, to dress and eat well, to travel. His first reaction is to resent his earnings being taxed away, and there is a temptation for politicians to abet him in his resentment in order to win his support. But on the other hand lie all the claims of the community – better education, better towns, better social services and so on through a long list of needs which can only be met through the public purse. To finance them there must be more public expenditure; which means more taxation. The issue is plain. (Abrams and Rose 1960: 114)

Similarly, Richard Crossman continued to argue that '... a truly democratic society cannot be achieved without shifting the balance between private and public consumption in order to provide as of right to every citizen those essential services which for far too long remained the privilege of a small economic class' (Crossman 1969).

The concern for social justice, linked to the greater aim of modernising Britain, was reiterated in 1966. Evidence of this commitment was the increase in pensions and benefits which was carried out within the first six months of office, the abolition of prescription charges and the attack on evictions from privately rented accommodation. A Ministry of Social Security was envisaged which would have the obligation 'to seek out and alleviate poverty whether among children or old people'. In welfare or community services, priority would be given to the old.

Some of Labour's reluctance to be seen as the party which would raise taxes had given way by the mid-sixties to the theme that if the public wanted better social services, they would have to be prepared to pay for them. But it was hoped that if taxes were distributed more fairly this would be acceptable if combined with increased prosperity. 'The way to pay for social progress is through a fairer system of taxes and a faster rate of economic expansion.' (Northcott 1964: 13) An attack on tax allowances and tax-free fringe benefits was advocated for they 'probably cost the Government more than £2,500 million a year – that is, far more than the National Insurance scheme and all the public health and welfare services combined' (op. cit.: 40).

One of the major items of Labour's social policy became that of comprehensive social security, for society was seen as divided between those who had adequate social security through private or occupational insurance and those who did not, again a policy of more appeal to those in secure employment. The idea of some kind of tax-credit scheme began to be put forward, although the mechanics of this had not been clearly worked out. It was hoped to use Inland Revenue tax returns to assess an individual's right to a guaranteed minimum income. However, Labour's ambivalence was not the only reason why this particular policy was not carried out. As important was the resistance of the Inland Revenue, partly because of technical difficulties and partly because its administrative conservatism objected to viewing taxation as a system of welfare distribution. Labour's morale and support declined in the period 1966 to 1969. Economic questions dominated and disillusionment set in among Labour's local party activists. The imposition of public expenditure cuts in July 1966 (£500 million package), the wages freeze (July 1966 to January 1967), the period of 'severe restraint' (February 1967 to July 1969) and increasing unemployment strained the patience of Labour supporters. Some left the Party or exerted their energies elsewhere. The Research Department began to attempt a move towards what they saw as a more radical position. This involved no new initiatives in policy but a more forceful presentation of socialist views and a comparison between the actions of Government and the policies of the Party. Social benefits would have to be paid for by higher taxation. 'The need to spend more on social services has meant that none of us can have this money in our pockets as well. Restraint in this direction is the inevitable price we are paying for progress on the social front.' (*Britain: Progress and Change*, the mid-term manifesto presented to the Labour Party Conference, October 1968.)

The National Executive Committee (NEC) document, *Agenda for a Generation*, included proposals which had emanated from the Research Department in the form of a discussion document, *Labour's Social Strategy*. But the Labour leaders felt themselves to be more in touch with the opinions of the electorate, who would be unwilling to pay higher taxes for increased social benefits. Roy Jenkins commented, 'we should look forward to expanding public services – certainly they are vitally necessary – but expanding them roughly in line with and not ahead of the growth in national income' (Labour Conference Report 1969: 253). 'We certainly ought not to be a party of taxation for taxation's sake or a party which is instinctively hostile to private consumption.' (ibid.) Similarly, Denis Healey felt Labour had to change its image in the context of the affluent society and the decline of working-class consciousness: 'Two things have struck me as a Leeds' MP. Eight of the Labour Clubs in my constituency have recently acquired new premises of palatial splendour – their only defect is a lack of parking space. When I go into these clubs on a Saturday night, four of five complaints are that income tax is too high and that we should not pay out so much in family allowances.' (*Socialist Commentary* November 1969) The State should therefore be concerned with 'pockets of distress' leaving the majority free to spend their extra earnings as they chose.

After 1966, the Labour Government struggled to maintain an accord with the trade unions while attempting to implement its policies of economic management. The aim was to build up the role of Government, to act positively and take the initiative within the system of corporate bias that had prevailed since the War. But the opposition of the unions was too great and the result for the Labour party was the disillusionment and alienation of all sections. The Government's strategy fell ultimately in disarray with appeal to the reactions of public opinion, as measured in polls or in comments in bars and clubs, becoming the touchstone of policy decisions. The justification for pragmatism had been the pursuit of political stability and economic growth. As economic growth remained elusive and political stability was threatened, it became transparently clear that the lack of principles to guide the direction of pragmatic policies had reduced the Government's actions to a neurotic obsession with the Party's image in public opinion.

That this had not been obvious from the start reflects the fact that Wilson appeared in the early 1960s to offer an alternative to the wrangles that had divided the Party in the thirteen years in the wilderness. The policy of positive economic management appeared to provide the basis for an integration of the conflicting interests within the Party and also to offer a viable platform on which to appeal to the voters, especially to the growing number of white-collar and affluent workers.

The failure of the strategy, which depended for its success on trade union reform and wages policy (both proving unobtainable), led the Government back to the politics of crisis management and the worries over the balance of payments and public expenditure which have dogged the post-war British economy. The key issue in social policy in this period was that of family poverty, impressed on government through contacts between the poverty lobby and sympathetic members of the Cabinet. The technical solution to this problem was, as it has always been, the paying of adequate family allowances on a universal basis. But the need to restrain public expenditure to satisfy the financial interests, whose clearest spokesman was the Treasury, and the traditional opposition to family allowances of trade unionists, made the resolution of this issue impossible within the existing balance of forces. Cabinet discus-

sions on the issue were protracted and agonised. The social demo-
crats within the party wanted, as a matter of conscience, to do something about growing poverty, but there was little real support for
these policies, and poverty never became a dominant question at
Labour Party conferences. It was the Fabian, professional lobby
that kept it alive as an issue, skilfully using their contacts with the
press and television and playing on the consciences of the intellectuals in the Cabinet. But the lack of interest of trade unions was
crucial as they concentrated on the more immediate issue of resist-
ing an encroachment on union power.

As for the electorate, it did not show any major concern with
family poverty in the 1960s. In surveys carried out in this period to
determine what the public thought were the major issues facing the
Government, family poverty was rarely mentioned. Public opinion
was increasingly opposed to higher social spending in general,
reflecting the increasing burden of taxation on the working class as
the tax threshold crept steadily down the social scale. The
public did indeed increasingly prefer the option of tax cuts to more
spending on the social services. Family allowances in particular
were a vote-loser, and it was manual workers rather than non-
manual workers who were opposed to them.

Eventually the technical solution of 'clawback' was adopted,
which drew on suggestions made by the Child Poverty Action Group
(CPAG) further refined by Nicholas Kaldor, the special tax adviser
to the Chancellor of the Exchequer, in a form which protected the
standard rate taxpayer. The principle was one of a shift from tax
allowances to a flat-rate benefit and was devised in such a way as to
ensure that the tax increase paid by the standard rate taxpayer was
exactly the same as the increase in family allowance. Keith G. Banting, in his thorough account of the period, makes the useful point
that: 'From the Inland Revenue's point of view, clawback was not a
sophisticated use of the tax system to concentrate benefit on real
need; it was a universal increase in family allowance primarily
financed through an inequitable tax increase on all families.' (Banting 1979: 95) This was based on the view of the tax system as solely
a revenue-raising system, in contrast to Titmuss' view that it can
operate as a form of indirect welfare distribution. In the light of
developments since the 1960s, however, which have seen a redistribution of income away from families to the childless and the
single, the Inland Revenue may now be seen to have been more
realistic in its assessment than it is usually given credit for being.

Jim Callaghan, who increasingly acted as the spokesman of the trade union voice in Cabinet arguments, insisted that the choice was between a universal increase in family allowances and a means-tested benefit. The aim to finance increasing social expenditure from economic growth – equality without tears – was becoming increasingly unrealistic. He commented that the political problem was to balance the social needs of the community with its willingness to accept the consequential burdens of taxation. 'He sensed the current of public opinion turning against social spending and in favour of tax cuts and he argued that middle-income, including skilled manual workers, were unwilling to sacrifice their standard of living so that social security could be improved.' (Banting 1979: 97) But while party tradition was still an influence in the discussions, electoral consequences were working in the opposite direction. The result was a token gesture towards increasing family allowances but the rejection of proposals for major reform.

In spite of the constraints of economic stagnation and the balance of payments crises of the 1960s, under Labour government there was some reduction in inequalities in the distribution of income. More importantly, the share of the national income collected by Government in taxation rose substantially, from 32 per cent to 43 per cent. Benefits were increased and the real disposable income of those relying wholly or mainly on benefits rose, but by how much was the subject of a rather acrimonious exchange between the CPAG and David Ennals. Family allowances were doubled, restoring them to their value in 1948. However, the operation of 'clawback', by which child tax allowances were reduced, meant that only a part of the increase in family allowance was a real increase. Significantly, the number of unemployed rose, which had to be seen as a loss of welfare. Reviewing these years, A. B. Atkinson concluded:

1. The claims made for the increase in aggregate 'effort' in the field of social security expenditure under the Labour Government were exaggerated. A substantial part of the rise in spending was attributable to there being more old people and more unemployed.
2. In 1965 there was a definite increase in the level of national insurance benefits, but in the next five years they scarcely kept pace with rising earnings. The periods between reviews of the benefit levels were shorter than under the Conservatives, but there was still a substantial fall in the purchasing power of benefits between reviews.
3. The introduction of supplementary benefits has not had the success claimed for it by Labour ministers and has failed to eliminate the problem of people not claiming the benefits to which they are entitled.

4. The gain to low income families from the 1968 rise in family allowances has largely been offset by higher national insurance contributions and income tax.
5. National superannuation would have led to a considerable increase in pensions but the gestation period was long and more could have been done to ease the burden of contributions on the low paid worker. (Atkinson 1972: 24)

Labour's big initiative in social policy, the earnings-related scheme of social security, gave little help to the low-paid and those outside the workforce. Most of the increase in social expenditure of those years was due to forces outside the Government's control, 'automatic' increases, due to growing numbers qualifying although, in that they did choose to meet these demands rather than cut provision, they could be seen as acting in accord with social democratic philosophy. Labour's pension plan, while not radically redistributive, had a distinct bias towards the lower-paid. It could be argued that, given the constraints of the public's unwillingness to pay more in taxes, Labour did as much as could be expected.

By 1970, a distinction between the policies of the two main parties was rather hard to see. Although changes were going on within the Conservative Party, these had not been picked up by the voters. Both parties seemed to agree on the need for a mixed economy, Welfare State, more planning and entry into the EEC. The leadership of the Labour Party proposed similar policies to those of the Conservatives by stressing that the main concern of social policy in the future should be with the needs of minority groups, of the 'socially handicapped', implying selective measures.

Having lost the election, Labour set up more than 50 study groups of widely composed membership, to prepare fresh party policies and be better prepared for the next election and for taking office. Consultations took place with experts and pressure-groups, including the CPAG. The Party recognised its neglect of social issues and aimed to strengthen its commitment in this area. In 1973, a policy document was produced which was decidedly more radical than many of the statements of the 1960s. The 'decline of working-class consciousness', which had in the fifties and sixties been thought to provide the political context within which the Party had to operate, seemed to have been refuted by the display of trade union opposition to industrial reform, the increasing militancy of shop stewards and the activities of public sector unions and interest groups like Tenants' Associations and the Claimants' Union. Labour's aims were now stated to be to achieve 'a fundamental and irreversible shift in the balance of power and wealth in favour of working people and their families', 'greater economic equality in income, wealth and living standards', the elimination of poverty and measures to 'make power in industry genuinely accountable to the workers and the community'. Here social policy reflected the interests of the working population. It was not based solely on altruism, and the key element in the programme was redistribution, redistribution of power, rewards and benefits. Again the old were singled out for favourable treatment with the promise to raise old-age pensions.

The marked shift in the stance of the Labour Party in these years resulted from a deliberate attempt to revive the alliance with the trade unions which had been ruptured by the fight over indus-trial relations and incomes policy in the late 1960s. A public act of contrition was exacted from the Labour leaders who were reminded of their dependence on the trade union movement, more especially so after the decline of the individual membership of the Party during the 1960s. The revived alliance was labelled 'the social contract'. It was initiated by Jack Jones when at the 1971 Confer-ence he said, 'There is no reason at all why a joint policy cannot be worked out. But let us have the closest possible liaison.' The aim was quite clearly to reassert the situation which had been estab-lished in the 1940–45 Government which had reflected the growing economic power of the trade unions and which Professor Samuel Beer had referred to in his book, *Modern British Politics*, as a new 'social contract', a term subsequently popularised by Harold Wil-son (Beer 1965: 215).

In January 1973, a new Liaison Committee of six members from the shadow Cabinet, six from the NEC and six from the TUC, produced a policy statement, *Economic Policy and the Cost of Liv-ing*. Among the measures proposed were control of basic food prices through subsidies, subsidization of public transport fares, the public ownership of land for building purposes, a large scale redistribution of income and wealth, the phasing out of social ser-vices charges and an immediate commitment to pension increases.

Back in office, however, the endemic problems of the British economy made a nonsense of these proposals. Financial pressures forced the new Government to retract on their commitments to the unions. The continuing deterioration of sterling forced the Labour Government to turn to the International Monetary Fund (IMF) for help. The terms of the loan granted entailed cuts in the Public Sector Borrowing Requirement (PSBR) of £1,000 million in

1977/78 and of £1,500 million in 1978/79. The major reason for the inadequacy of the social contract was its failure to include any discussion of incomes policy – the issue had been carefully avoided when the contract was being drawn up. But incomes policy is vital for the solution of these economic problems and its omission from the social contract leads to the suspicion that the agreement was mainly a cynical device to gain both trade union and electoral support. In spite of these failures however, through the social contract, the TUC exerted more influence over the Labour Government in 1974–79 than in previous years. Yet the 'winter of discontent' of 1978–79 may not unfairly be said to have contributed in large part to the dismissal of the Labour Government in 1979. The revolt of the dispossessed and unrepresented below and of the affluent workers above played havoc with the TUC's own attempt to represent, contain and centralise the very divergent forces now existing under the heading of 'trade unionists'. The revolt of militant shop stewards in the post-war years had led to the radicalisation of the trade union leadership, but the attempt to represent the conflicting aims of the low-paid and highly-paid skilled workers, of workers in the private and the public sectors, of men and women workers, of those in the declining North and those in the prosperous South under one banner – and at a time of recession and falling living standards – placed too heavy a strain on both trade union leadership and political institutions.

Simply to condemn the last Labour Government in such a situation for its 'abandonment of its traditional concern with equality' is not enough. Exhortations to remember socialism have long proved inadequate. The pressures placed on governments attempting to resolve these problems are immense.

The Labour Government of 1974–79 was far from dangerously egalitarian in spite of Denis Healey's promise to 'squeeze the rich till the pips squeaked'. The early pay policies achieved some improvement in the relative position of the bottom tenth but this was slight and began to wane in later years. The Government did attempt to protect the poor against the effects of inflation and pensioners in particular improved their position relative to take-home pay. The Conservative proposal to link pensions to prices would have given a smaller rise in pensions over the period 1974–79. The two major reforms carried through were those for pensions and child benefits – the situation of single-parent families and the long-term unemployed did not improve.

To some extent, therefore, some sections of the poor were protected. But public expenditure cuts set in train before the IMF laid down its conditions, the abandonment of the aim of full employment and most notably the failure to implement a wealth tax have to be set against these slight achievements. When Labour took office in February 1974, unemployment was half a million. When they left in March 1979, the total unemployed was one and a quarter million. The average cut in the standard of living between 1974 and 1977 was 7 per cent. The disposable incomes of families with four children was cut by a chilling 20 per cent (Bosanquet and Townsend 1980).

The Conservative Party's post-war reactions to social and economic developments had been at first to accommodate to the Welfare State and then for a while to flirt with policies of economic management. The electoral pressures of consensus politics led the Party to reach out to the middle ground with policies aimed at wooing the young, white-collar, scientific, technical and managerial group. But with the failure of the politics and economics of collaboration, the opposition grew stronger. During the sixties, Conservative Party Central Office worked out policies based on free-market ideas. The acceptance of these proposals by a sufficient number of the voters in 1979 established a Government in power with a 'mandate' from the people to pursue more vigorously the policies which had been reluctantly adopted by its Labour predecessors. The claims of the poor have not been central to Conservative Party thinking but have merely figured as part of electoral strategy in trying to win over the pensioner lobby. Conservative Governments have followed the advice of civil servants in adopting practical solutions to social problems, with the aim of achieving stability. And social policies have been used astutely to argue for the efficiency of selective systems, thus encouraging the dominance of the free market as the first principle of government.

In the 1940s, the Conservative Party's attitude to welfare was distrusted by the electorate. In 1942, when Beveridge produced his plan, Churchill did not like it. When the plan was presented to the House, Sir John Anderson explained that while the Government accepted its provisions in principle, there could be no binding commitment. In this debate, arguments were voiced against the Report mainly by Tories. However, the Tory Reform Group of which Quintin Hogg (Lord Hailsham) was a leading member vigorously supported proposals for social security reform. An amendment demanding prompt legislation was defeated by 338 votes to

121. With two exceptions, all Labour members not in office voted for the amendment. Most Tories voted against. However, it is interesting to note that the Labour leaders supported Churchill in this and Ernest Bevin was apparently so angered by this revolt of Labour backbenchers that he refused to attend meetings of the PLP from February 1943 to May 1944 (Taylor 1978).

So the view held by the electorate that Labour stood for social security legislation while the Conservatives were against it was a fair one. In the debate 'the opponents of the Report ... spoke as if the basis of the Report were an attempt to cadge money off the rich on behalf of the not entirely deserving poor'. Tom Hopkinson commented, 'The fear that small children or old age pensioners may take to drink or gambling is a very real one to a large section of the Conservative Party.' (*Picture Post* 6 March 1943)

After its defeat in 1945, the Conservative Party had to adjust to the changed reality of politics. 'If the Conservative Party had followed Hayekian policies after the war, it would have become like the old European Liberal parties.' (Gilmour 1978: 119) The Party adapted to the prevailing conditions and values and, led by Lord Woolton and R.A. Butler, geared its policies towards social and industrial issues. The Conservatives' ability to adapt allowed them to retain their place in the two-party system which has characterised British politics. The Tories convinced the electorate, as R.A. Butler had hoped, that they had a policy 'which was viable, efficient and humane, which would release and reward enterprise and initiative but without abandoning social justice or reverting to mass unemployment' (Butler 1973: 132). Ian Gilmour summarises the Conservative political stance since 1945 thus:

general welcome of the welfare state, though such acceptance does not preclude alteration, improvement or pruning; full employment, however defined, as a prime aim of economic policy; the encouragement of ownership of property; the acceptance of trade unions as an important estate of the realm coupled with the recognition that many of the activities of trade unionism are economically damaging, and lately, constitutionally unjustifiable; the conviction that Britain must play her proper part both militarily and diplomatically in the defence of the West; the belief that the mixed economy is a condition both of political freedom and of social stability; the judgement that private enterprise is not only essential to the preservation of political freedom but also when applicable the most efficient form of economic organisation, coupled with the recognition that here as in other countries the state is bound to play an important part in the economy. (Gilmour 1978: 19)

Conservatives claim to abhor poverty as much as do Socialists. Where they differ however is in their views on the causes of poverty and the best way to attack it. They deny that policies should aim to reduce inequality, and say that these would only make the plight of the poor much worse. This view sees social groups connected together as in a train. As the leaders (the engine) make progress so the rest are pulled up and along behind. The relation of the guard's van to the engine will not change but all will have moved up the hill. To attack inequality is to attack the initiative and enterprise on which everyone's success depends. 'The incentive of inequality, if inequality corresponds to skill and energy, is one of the main means whereby new wealth can be created and active characters spurred on to produce of their best – to the great advantage of mankind at large.' The 'raising up of humanity from the depths of the primeval mire' is a great advance which has been the result of brains and opportunity working together, 'stimulated into action by the ordinary and homely motive of striving to win something better for one's family than has been known in the past' (Hailsham 1959: 110). Thus what Britain needs is 'an Opportunity State to match and sustain the Welfare State' (op. cit.: 112). Conservatives are against the State adopting the role of Grand Almoner although they recognise that the Welfare State is here to stay, and as one commented, 'You can't shoot Santa Claus'.

The Conservative Case in 1959 was put thus by Viscount Hailsham.

Conservatives believe that the right way forward is not through a system of equality, under which the state would provide social services for all, but through a system of equality of opportunity, under which men would be free to make self-respecting social provision for themselves as far as their work and their worth allowed, leaving the resources of the State to cope ever more generously with those individuals who cannot provide for themselves and those services which no individual can provide for himself. (Hailsham 1959: 114)

Sir Ian Gilmour, writing almost twenty years later, reiterated this view but pointed to some of the reservations Conservatives were voicing about the expansion of social services in post-war years.

State provision for welfare is fully in accordance with Conservative principles. The welfare state is a thoroughly Conservative institution, which is why Conservatives did so much to bring it into existence; and its roots go deep in English history. Beyond doubt, the balance now needs to be redressed. More and more money has been poured into the social services and increasing numbers of people have been employed in them without much discernible improvement at least recently in the quality of the service provided. Moreover the object of state benefit and state welfare is to do for the individual what he cannot do for himself. Increasingly, however, under Labour Governments state welfare has become an end in itself, and a means of preventing the individual from satisfying his own wants. That is prohibitively expensive, damaging to the economy, socially harmful, and a threat to freedom. The social wage must not be allowed to turn our people into wage slaves. The welfare state must be pruned in places, and pruning will strengthen it like roses. More private provision must be encouraged, and private competition with public services has economic as well as social advantages. Yet in the present state of industrial society, public welfare on a large scale is inescapable. (Gilmour 1978: 152)

These have been consistent themes in British Conservatism. Where Labour's discussions of poverty and welfare have been set within statements about social justice, inequality, redistribution of income, fair taxation, public expenditure, and compassion for the social casualties, Conservatives talk of enterprise, initiative, incentives, freedom, choice, equality of opportunity, efficiency and cutting taxes.

In 1945 they promised to implement the social security plans discussed in 1944, accepted responsibility for the maintenance of a high and stable level of employment and also aimed to cut taxes. Familiar themes began to emerge at the 1950 election. Government expenditure was attacked and the promise made to reduce taxation. The Socialists had 'spread the tale that social welfare is something to be had from the State free, gratis and for nothing'. 'In order to lower taxes and the high cost of living we must cut down government spending', which would help to restore incentive and, they warned 'Britain can only enjoy the social services for which she is prepared to work'. The fear that the Welfare State was too cosy, featherbedding the people, was voiced. A change of direction in policy would maintain a solid base below which no-one would fall but 'above which each must be encouraged to rise to the utmost limit of his ability'. 'We shall foster the ancient virtue of personal thrift.' Free enterprise was emphasised again in 1951 and the mismanagement and inefficiency of State-run ventures criticised. A Conservative Government would 'cut out all unnecessary Government expenditure, simplify the administrative machine and prune waste and extravagance in every department'. The best way to preserve the social services would be to increase the national output. 'We cannot possibly keep ourselves alive without the individual effort, invention, contrivance, thrift and good housekeeping of our people.' (Election manifesto 1950)

The restriction of government's responsibility to that of maintaining a basic standard of living which all are 'free to rise above as far as their industry and talents may take them' has been a constant motif in Conservative manifestos. Social security and social services should not be used to·'level down', they should not be a 'substitute for family thrift'.

During the fifties Labour attacked the Conservative record in office – saying they had allowed the health and welfare services to decline and poverty to increase in spite of growing affluence. The Conservatives countered this in 1959 by emphasising the reforming elements in their programme. A 'modern pensions plan' had been initiated ('modern' referred to graduated contributions); Macmillan's personal interest in ameliorating local unemployment had encouraged retraining and mobility of labour; local authorities would be helped to develop further their social services and the training of social workers would be promoted. Protecting their Achilles' heel, the Government reminded the electorate that pensions had been increased three times. Pensioners would continue to be protected and would share in the 'good things which a steadily expanding economy will bring'. Policies to improve the situation of widowed mothers, the disabled and the poor were also mentioned.

The Conservatives had to some extent stolen Labour's clothes (or, as Macmillan put it, their Wykehamite ties) by introducing their pension scheme prior to the election. Criticism of the scheme, that it aimed mainly to reduce the Exchequer subsidy and favoured the better off, were rather technical and hard for the public to grasp. The Conservatives thus cleverly spiked Labour's big gun. However, the interest in pensions was also a response to an awareness of the growing cost of old-age pensions as the proportion of the old in the population steadily rose. The concentration by Governments of both parties on this issue for 20 years indicates that this is largely a technical problem, rather than one of great ideological significance. Each party tried to direct its policy in ways consistent with the general aims of 'incentives' or 'redistribution', but the necessity for *some* policy on old-age pensions was unavoidable.

The acceptance of the Welfare State and of the special relationship with the trade unions by the Tory Party reflected the ascendancy of the Reform Group and politicians like Butler, Macmillan and Hogg, and later Heath, Macleod and Gilmour. Macmillan's Government in 1962 tried to act more forcefully in the pursuit of economic management, to win the agreement of the trade unions to wage regulation in return for a recognition of their corporate power. But this position was never fully accepted; there was always a current of opinion in favour of radical free enterprise. This opposition became open revolt in 1957 when Peter Thorneycroft, as Chancellor, challenged the existing assumptions. With Enoch Powell and Nigel Birch, Thorneycroft was forced to resign and the implicit contract with labour was renewed. But Thorneycroft did not give up. Through his influence within the Conservative Party, he worked to win over a new generation of Conservatives to his ideas, ideas that gradually gained strength within the Party during the 1960s. Edward Heath's attempt to put them into practice in 1970 was defeated by events but the battle was renewed in 1979 when Mrs Thatcher came to power, challenging the old orthodoxy.

While in opposition in the 1960s, the Party moved further away from acceptance of statism. The Selsdon doctrine was publicised in 1969 and presented as the Conservatives' alternative proposals. The origins of what in the 1970s was to become a 'radical attack' on poverty must be placed within the general framework of the attack on consensus politics.

In the 1964 election, when social issues were important, the Conservative Party had reiterated the argument that social services and concern for the poor and handicapped were not the prerogatives of Labour. As had happened with discussion of old-age pensions in 1959, the Conservatives in 1964 proposed a similar scheme to Labour's, one for earnings-related unemployment and sickness benefit. Thus the major innovations to the social security scheme which occurred in the 1960s were ones on which both parties agreed. Roughly similar plans were proposed by each and since the details would be worked out by civil servants in consultation with interested pressure groups, the large degree of consensus which existed is clear. Debate was concerned with detailed arguments as to which scheme would be most generous to whom. Similarly, discussion of the value of social security benefits, by how much they had been increased, how often, whether keeping pace with prices or earnings, formed a key point of dispute in election campaigns, with each party claiming superiority in benevolence and efficiency. Governments demonstrated their concern by raising benefits and pensions in the months running up to the election – so much so that this could indicate the likelihood of an election being called, and led J.C. Kincaid to comment that the single most useful strategy for improving the living standards of old-age pensioners would be to hold more frequent elections.

The Conservatives, however, continued to stress the importance of concentrating resources on those most in need, not wasting them on those who could look after themselves, a view which Labour was increasingly coming to accept. This theme was evident in 1966. Efforts should be made to develop a fresh pattern of social priorities – 'to see more generous help for those who have special needs not yet met by the Welfare State'. 'Give more generous help to children in families where the income is below minimum need, to the *very* old, to the *chronic* sick, to the *severely* disabled and to others *most* in need'. (my italics) 'Those most in need should get the most help.' (Conservative Manifesto 1966) The implication that family responsibility was somehow undermined by the provision of universal social services had long been an undercurrent in Conservative thinking. The Welfare State had turned the people into 'moral pygmies'. Parents failed to plan ahead or provide for themselves and their children, thus detracting from an attitude of responsibility towards family commitments and contributing to the wasteful manner in which those services were being used.

However, in spite of the rhetoric, the actual policies proposed by the Conservatives were barely distinguishable from those of the Labour Party. Occupational pension schemes should be encouraged, together with proposals for the transferability of pension rights. Labour's major reform creating the DHSS, for which so much was claimed at the time, is also promised in the Conservative election manifesto of 1966, combining the Ministry of Health, the Ministry of Pensions and National Insurance and the National Assistance Board into a single Department with local officers who would have a positive duty to seek out 'those needing help whether in cash or care. The new department would have a research organisation to pinpoint changing needs'. What both parties were proposing were solutions to social problems on which there was general agreement that something should be done. That their solutions were so similar indicates how little of the initiative for reform came from within the parties themselves. Policy proposals actually emanated from pressure groups, experts and civil servants. Both parties responded to these pressures as far as was consistent with the public mood, which favoured more selective social services rather than increased taxation.

Since Conservative Party policy had been redirected along the lines advocated by R.A. Butler and Labour Party policy had followed the revisionist or social democratic signposts, some Conservatives claimed that it was difficult to get a distinctive party image across to the electorate. 'It was much easier in 1945–51 when we at least had some socialism to attack.' (quoted in Butler and Pinto-Duschinsky 1971: 63) Others felt the Conservative Party had moved too far to the left and that the Conservative Reform Group and Bow Group had exerted too great an influence on party thinking. In 1961, a group of right-wingers had formed the Monday Club hoping to redress the balance. Similarly PEST (Pressure for Economic and Social Toryism) and the Institute of Economic Affairs (IEA) forcefully and insistently argued the themes of *laissez-faire*, greater economic radicalism, reduction of government interference and the issue of private welfare.

In formulating their new policies, the Conservative Party was responding to what it perceived to be changes in what the public wanted and in society. The grass-roots of the party made insistent demands to improve the position of small business, but it was the burden of taxation which proved to be the most salient and divisive issue in the late 1960s, with public reaction provoked by the combined effects of inflation, fiscal drag and the erosion of allowances.

Policy advisory groups set to work between 1966 and 1970, thoroughly reviewing Conservative Party policy in many areas, including national insurance, health and social security. The free-marketeers in the party advocated drastic cuts in taxation, even though this would necessitate a reduction in welfare benefits. They argued that spending on the social services should be reduced, although not in areas of greatest need. This policy accorded with Conservative views but it was felt it could be electorally unpopular. However, between the late 1960s and mid 1970s, increased publicity was given to 'scroungers' and 'malingerers'. The issue of social security for the dependents of strikers received prominence, being mentioned in the 1970 Conservative Party election manifesto, and rising taxes and national insurance contributions hardened attitudes to welfare recipients.

The Conservatives pressed on with detailed studies of family poverty, of abuses of the social services, the problems of disincentives, proposals for a negative income tax and ways of reducing public expenditure. The introduction of selective welfare benefits was advocated to create a 'middle-income society with more aid for the poor' (*Financial Times*, 17 March 1970). Both parties now recognised that the choice was between lower taxes with fewer social services and higher taxes and higher benefits, but in 1970 neither party was willing to put the issue squarely before the electorate. The Conservatives still stressed growth as the best way to help the poor, but by 1979 they were ready to state their new beliefs more openly. The electorate, at least the middle-income electorate of the south-east of England, chose the option of lower taxes, fewer services and reduced benefits. The interests of the working population in the different regions clearly diverged on this issue.

The main social security proposal worked out in opposition in the sixties by the Conservative Party was for a tax-credit scheme. In power, Heath's Government produced Green Papers on Value Added Tax (VAT) and on the tax-credit scheme, and a Select Committee was set up to discuss the latter. The main effective opposition to the Conservative scheme came not from the pressure-groups, although CPAG was loudly critical, but from the Inland Revenue Staff Federation who argued that it was unworkable. It was this opposition from the administration which led to the reversal of this initiative. It was replaced by the Family Income Supplement (FIS), a plan which had the advantage of supporting the principle of selectivism. But FIS itself originated within the civil service: it had been worked out by civil servants in the 1960s during the long and tortured discussions on family allowances.

Between 1970 and 1974, the Conservatives reformed taxation arrangements and introduced tax cuts. They did not carry through their promise to CPAG to raise family allowances but introduced FIS instead. Routine reviews of pensions were established. Free school milk was curtailed.

Two innovations have been made in social security by government in the post-war years which stand out among a number of less significant reforms. The first is the introduction of the earnings-related principle to which Labour lays claim, although similar proposals were made by the Conservatives. The second is the introduction of more selective benefits in the early 1970s, especially the Family Income Supplement. The implementation of these measures reflects Conservative Party ideology and especially the personal influence of Sir Keith Joseph.

The seizing of the initiative by the Conservatives reflected their awareness of the political situation and an ability to capitalize on it. FIS was an ideal scheme for them, because public opinion favoured selective services for the deserving and harsh measures for the work-shy. These social security proposals could be used to 'beat the general drum of selectivity' (quoted in Banting 1979: 76). The success of FIS usefully promoted the ideas of the free marketeers and with that the wider monetarist and selectivist policies they favoured. The initiative was also politically astute. It fed on and encouraged splits within the Labour movement. The success and popularity of these policies exposed the inadequacy of the Labour Government's response and the contradiction between its economic management strategies and its rhetoric of social reform. It highlighted the failure of trade unions to improve the situation of the low-paid and their concern to protect 'differentials'. By giving money to the low-paid, it might also be possible to head off some of the steam building up in support of disruptive activity by public sector unions, and it was in keeping with what the civil service wanted to see. The impact of the selectivist policies also encouraged the divisions within the working class which have increasingly prevented the formation of a class-based alternative to Conservative policies.

Because of the impact of Sir Keith Joseph at the DHSS during Edward Heath's administration, the Conservatives had overtaken Labour by the 1974 election as the party thought 'best able to handle' the issue of pensions and benefits. So Labour's identification with aid for the needy – such an important part of its image – had been undermined. Increases to basic pension rates, a £10 Christmas bonus, special benefits for the over-eighties, for widows with young children, those widowed between the ages of forty and fifty and most significantly the Family Income Supplement had had an impact on public opinion.

Discussion of social policy issues helped also in the more vigorous promotion of the Conservative alternative in the years of opposition between 1974 and 1979. If the new political and economic policies were to be accepted, something would have to give from the incompatible triad of the consensus period: full employment, price stability and rising living standards. The choice to throw out the aim of full employment was made by both parties and politicians took up the issue of 'scrounging' as part of the manoeuvre to get this accepted. The issue of scroungers defrauding 'the welfare' played an important part in the attempt to encourage an acceptance of higher rates of unemployment than the two or three per cent of the 1950s. In a major speech at Preston in September 1975, Sir Keith Joseph argued the free-market line, that unemployment should be allowed to find its 'natural' level without government interference, which only led to inflation; and he claimed that if unemployment statistics were calculated more carefully, the apparent numbers would be reduced. Among the numbers presently counted as unemployed, he said, are 'scroungers, unemployables and people who will not make their share of the effort, who expect the government or their fellow men to do everything for them' (*The Times*, 25 September 1975: 5).

Conservative Party social policy has been consistent, advocating the State's responsibility for basic provision but individual responsibility for higher benefits and better services. True to their tradition of responding to the public mood, their promotion of these issues has varied. So long as the mixed economy and Welfare State were electorally popular, its policies aimed at their maintenance. As public opinion changed with increasing resentment of trade unions and taxation, Conservative policy responded. Powerful voices have preached the message of the free market and most of them have aligned themselves with the Conservative Party. As these ideas, particularly with reference to monetary policy, gained ground in influential circles in the Press, the civil service and the country, the Conservative Party responded and clearly and cogently offered new policies. In the field of social welfare, these involved selective welfare benefits generous to the needy but with firmer treatment for 'malingerers' or strikers and their families, advocacy of charges for certain services as a way to control demand and raise revenue, private health and welfare schemes, occupational pensions, a greater role for voluntary effort in community care, greater inequalities of income to act as incentives to enterprise and risk-taking, and tax cuts. A firm stress on the role of money as the arbiter of decisions was followed through in 1979 with immediate income tax cuts and an onslaught on the social services and social security benefits.

These policies probably won Mrs Thatcher the 1979 election. The polarization of the parties reflected a polarization of the electorate. It was not, however, clearly divided along traditional class lines. The conflict was between those with an interest in *statism* and those with an interest in the *free market*. Statism was supported by those dependent on the State for benefits, subsidies, employment and services. The free market was supported by those in profitable private industries and those who were able, or felt able, to look after their educational, health and social welfare through private expenditure.

In their 1980 budget, the Conservatives laid out their strategy for the remainder of their term of office: child benefits would be raised from November 1980 by 75p, less than the rise in inflation (a small revolt by Conservative backbenchers soon faded away) and tax allowances were raised in line with inflation as required by the Rooker-Wise amendment. However, the lower 25 per cent band of taxation, instituted by the previous Labour Government to protect the lower-paid, was abolished. The effect of this was to raise tax allowances by about 11 per cent overall, less than the rise in prices, with particularly hard effects on the lower-paid. Earnings-related supplements to social security unemployment and sickness benefits would be abolished. Social security benefits would be taxed and strikers' families' claims for supplementary benefits reduced by £12. At the same time the very poor were protected, as pensions and long-term supplementary benefits rose in line with inflation. As with other of this Government's policies, the unemployed, the lower-paid and those with families bore the brunt of the squeeze: the bottom 10 per cent were protected but the 10 to 15 per cent band above them would be hardest hit and the effect of such policies would be to increase the numbers of claimants by pushing the lower-paid into poverty. The Conservative Government thus continued the trends which had characterised the post-war years. The Labour Party in Parliament could raise only token opposition to many of these changes since they followed the lines of those they had themselves pursued and had discussed in 1976. Only 40 members remained in the House to hear the details of the changes being spelt out by Mr Biffen. The Government's decisions won the approval of the public. A survey conducted by Market Opinion Research International (MORI) for the *Sunday Times* showed large proportions of the public favouring cuts in social security benefits as the best way to reduce public expenditure. Forty-three per cent thought social security benefits should be cut. Only 19 per cent, however, thought child benefits should be cut. In commenting on the Howe budget, a majority of 86 per cent thought he was right to increase old-age pensions and 32 per cent that he was right to reduce social security payments to strikers' families. Support for an attack on social security benefits was provided by the 62 per cent who still thought that 'many lower-paid people would be just as well off if they stopped working and lived on State benefits' (70 per cent had agreed with this in April 1978). Government was responding to the public mood and its policies could thus be justified.

The failure to produce an instant economic miracle by the rhetoric of incentives has produced some disillusion. The uncompromising attitude of Government, its deliberate attempt at a showdown with the trade unions and with public sector workers and the extreme speed at which a reversal of post-war trends was attempted, especially in the social services, led to opposition not only from the trade unions and those whose interests were best served by a form of statism, but also from elements within the Conservative Party who had not been convinced by the free-market proposals. The emphasis of these critics was not on economic failure. The economic policies of the Government were acceptable given the lack of a clear alternative, and were in any case in many ways similar to those which had been pursued less wholeheartedly by the previous Labour Government. The spectre which haunted them was that of political instability and great industrial unrest. Any attempt to change the political system was more likely to lead to trouble than the economic changes themselves.

Sir Ian Gilmour protested: 'In the Conservative view, economic liberation, à la Professor Hayek, because of its starkness and its failure to create a sense of community is not a safeguard of political freedom but a threat to it ... A free state will not survive unless its people feel loyalty to it. And they will not feel loyalty to it unless they gain from the State protection and other benefits. Lectures on the ultimate beneficence of competition and on the dangers of interfering with market forces will not satisfy people who are in trouble. If the State is not interested in them why should they be interested in the State?' (Gilmour 1980) Thus there are still voices to be heard within the Conservative Party urging the need to protect the Welfare State and not to erode it. The immediate future of the poor depends on the struggle within the Conservative Party between these two tendencies.

From a comparison of the programmes of the two major political parties in Britain today, it is clear that ideology has played a part in the formulation of their social policies and that there are consistent differences between the parties in their attitudes to key issues. Within each party there have been changes in the dominance of particular currents of thinking over these years. The social democratic view gained ascendancy in the Labour Party in the fifties. In the sixties, ideas of economic management dominated but gave way in the seventies. The ideas of the free market and monetarism came to prevail in the Conservative Party in the seventies. These changes have had some impact on the policies proposed for poverty and welfare. One can see, too, how each has been influenced by the programmes of the other. A party in opposition may exert an important influence on the policies of the governing party through its advocacy of certain policies and publicising of problem areas. Pressure from Labour encouraged the acceptance by the Conservatives of the Welfare State and prompted them to improve the situation of the social casualties to whose plight Labour had drawn attention. The transition towards advocacy of selective measures by Labour was partly under the influence of Tory criticisms of the waste and inefficiency of universal benefits. Each party influences the other by raising issues to which the Government of the day feels obliged to respond. Crucially, it limits the options open to the other after a change of Government in the 'inheritance' it leaves behind since the establishment of certain policies and institutions constrains the succeeding Government in that a radical upheaval may be undesirable. Although Labour had criticised FIS in opposition, they retained it when in power. The Conservatives have accepted much of Labour's pension plan, although Labour had thrown out the Conservatives' alternative plan when taking office in 1974. (However, the Conservative Government has altered one key part of the Labour plan – that to link pensions to rises in prices or earnings, whichever is the higher.)

While the logic of the argument so far is that a radical change in direction will take place in the 1980s following the final collapse of consensus politics and the agreed collaboration of industry, Government and trade unions, a word of caution should be introduced:

Incoming governments have spent their first year or two abolishing or drastically modifying the measures – often quite sensible – of their predecessors, and pressing ahead with the measures – often unrealistic or irrelevant – which they have formulated in opposition. (Stewart 1977: 241) By the end of the 1960s, for example, the Conservatives were talking as though there was scope for massive cuts in public expenditure without anybody getting hurt very much – conveniently ignoring the social, demographic and environmental realities which had caused irresistible demands for rising public expenditure. When they took office in 1970 they found that unless the whole fabric of the welfare state was to be destroyed – the political implications of which they were not willing to face – the scope for cuts was very limited. (op. cit.: 243) Labour, by contrast, tends to lose sight in opposition of the hard facts of public finance which it has painfully learnt in office, and to talk as though large increases in public expenditure can be painlessly met out of the fruits of faster growth. (ibid.)

Ministers in the Thatcher Cabinet, however, emphasised *ad nauseam* that this time there would be no U-turns, that they were willing to face up to the political implications of destroying the fabric of the Welfare State. Given this, the strength of pressure groups aiming to defend those institutions and protect the poor and weak would be of crucial importance.

Chapter seven
CHANNELS OF INFLUENCE

Richard Crossman believed that the most important problem facing those concerned with social policy is the 'ever increasing cost of the social services and the ever increasing resistance to paying for them' (Crossman 1969). He outlined three reasons for increases in public expenditure: *demographic change*, especially an increase in the numbers of old and young; *the levelling up of living standards*: 'During the period since I became an active socialist, Britain has been transformed into a community where the majority are affluent and only a minority are poor'; and lastly *technological change*. Political forces could have been added to his list. The two major political parties have often engaged in a process of competitive bidding – pensioneering – especially for the votes of the old and families: there are 8 million pensioners and 13 million parents of dependent children. Indeed, the poor have been identified by CPAG as 'the new Corporate Interest', although their votes have not as yet been effectively mobilized.

Governments are constrained in their actions by a number of factors, some of which were referred to by Crossman in October 1964 when, five days after assuming responsibility for housing, he wrote in his diary about 'the tremendous effort it requires not to be taken over by the civil service'. Other factors are the commitments of the previous Government, which may be difficult to reverse, or the reports of committees set up by their predecessors. Within the Cabinet, Ministers have to fight for their department. One effect of the amalgamation of Health and Social Security into one department was to give these interests a safe seat in the Cabinet. The appointment of Richard Crossman as Secretary of State at the same time, improved the relative bargaining power of this department. However, it may have detracted from ministerial control over civil servants for 'I realised by the end of the day that in claiming both

Health and Social Security, I've certainly taken on a challenge because it means mastering two completely different worlds' (Crossman 1977).

Ministers have to be especially well-versed in the political arts if they are to extract money from the Treasury. In Whitehall it is said, 'whoever wins the election, the Treasury always wins'. As Harold Wilson summed it up, in a final, rather impatient and dismissive letter to Brian Abel-Smith, Peter Townsend and Tony Lynes, who had protested at his Government's 'narrow and unimaginative approach to social policy' and long delays in fulfilling promises:

it is, of course, true that large increases in benefits of all kinds would help to eliminate need. But there are many competing claims and there is a limit to what we can do and the speed with which we can do it. We shall nevertheless, and of course, continue to pursue our social objectives as fast as the growing strength of the economy will permit, Yours sincerely, Harold Wilson, June 29 1967. (correspondence reprinted in, *Poverty* No 4 Autumn 1967: 13)

A pressure group can be defined as an organisation which tries to influence either national or local government regardless of which party is in power. It may be protective or promotional. Protective organisations act in the interests of one section or group in society. Promotional organisations aim to further a cause or idea. They can be called societies *of* and societies *for* particular interests. The usual tactic employed is that of *lobbying* and the more successful the pressure group, the better established its links with the executive, so much so that some of these pressure groups are now regularly consulted by Government about policy almost as an established part of constitutional practice. As Government has come to control greater areas of daily life, so there has been a parallel increase in pressure groups representing the interests of the 'clients' of the Welfare State. This may be viewed as a good or a bad thing: bad, where politicians and civil servants exercise patronage in discriminating between clients; good, if it provides 'new centres of democratic initiative outside the party system', especially where the party system fails to represent certain interests, like those of minority groups (Wootton 1978).

In assessing the influence of the various political forces, special attention will be paid to three issues: the *rediscovery of poverty, family allowances and scrounging.*

FORCES WORKING FOR THE POOR

In the rediscovery of poverty, a crucial part has been played by independent surveys and by the *redefinition* of poverty. Names prominent in this campaign will be familiar by now: Richard Titmuss, Peter Townsend, and Brian Abel-Smith, who together exercised an influence comparable to that of Tawney and Laski a generation before. The groups with which these three were associated indicate the network of allegiances and institutions which have at different times and in different ways promoted the cause of the poor: the Labour Party, the Fabian Society, the London School of Economics, the Child Poverty Action Group and university departments of Sociology and Social Administration.

In the rediscovery of poverty, the impact of Abel-Smith and Townsend's *The Poor and the Poorest* (1965) was of over-riding significance. The audience towards whom they directed most of their attention then was the Labour Movement. As committed socialists, in the 1950s and early 1960s they saw the Labour Party as the vehicle for social reform. Their essays in the volume *Conviction* (MacKenzie, ed.), published in 1958, were frequently quoted in discussions. Brian Abel-Smith, in the essay 'Whose Welfare State?', argued that the middle class had benefited disproportionately from the educational and health services. He discussed the differential impact of direct and indirect taxation, pointing out that 'the prestige-building of private enterprise puts to shame the grubby old institutions of welfare', and he anticipated the later arguments of the 1960s and 1970s which placed economic growth before welfare: '... action in this field must await improvement in the general financial situation and particularly in the balance of payments. Our prosperity depends upon a sound economy and any further expenditures on the welfare state will do more harm than good to the cause he has at heart.' To which he would have replied: 'Whose prosperity? Whose welfare state?' (Abel-Smith 1958: 73).

In the same volume, Peter Townsend made the same appeal to humane instincts and the fraternal impulse. He saw quite clearly who were his opponents and quoted the Director of the Conservative Political Centre, who had written in February 1958 on 'The Future of the Welfare State'. The Director had criticised 'squandering public money on providing indiscriminate benefits for citizens, many of whom do not need them and some of whom do not want them'. Townsend battled for universalism against the rising tide of selectivism. And he began to advocate his concept of 'relative poverty':

Beveridge took over the kind of measure used by those who had carried out surveys of poverty before the war. It looked bogus, was bogus and has been shown to be bogus . . . the unemployment and sickness benefits for a man in 1958 form a much smaller percentage of the average wage than they did in 1938 or indeed in 1912. (Townsend 1958: 100)

Peter Townsend has never been afraid to criticise. In the 1950s, he argued that Labour politicians had been happy to exaggerate the achievements of the Welfare State because they felt they could gain most of the credit. Later, in the 1960s, he was an outspoken critic of the Wilson administration. Although he became Professor of Sociology at Essex University, he has always stood to one side of the sociology Establishment. His view of sociology is above all 'studying very carefully the life of the poorest and most handicapped members of Society'. His calculation of the 'submerged fifth' was widely accepted and very influential. What stands out from his writing is a profound sympathy with and understanding of the life of the British working class – an empathy which has informed his suggestions for *workable* social policies. He affirmed his 'faith in people, in the fundamental goodness of man' and commented, 'these are generally regarded as being Christian virtues and yet they are the essence of Socialism' (MacKenzie 1958: 118).

When one looks at the list of 'Who's Who in the Child Poverty Action Group' in 1967, the names and institutions give some indication of the predominant influences in this period and their social bases:-

Chairman: A.F. Philp (Secretary of Family Service Units)
Hon. Secretary: Dr Harriet Wilson (University of Birmingham)
Hon. Treasurer: Walter Birmingham (Warden of Toynbee Hall)
Committee Members:
    Professor Brian Abel-Smith (London School of Economics)
    Mrs Margaret F. Bligh (National Council of Women)
    Mrs Audrey Harvey (writer and social worker)
    Miss Beti Jones (Glamorgan Children's Officer)
    Geoffrey Rankin (Islington Family Service Unit)
    Professor Peter Townsend (University of Essex)
    Des Wilson (Director of Shelter)
    John Veit Wilson (University of Essex)

Audrey Harvey's pamphlet *Casualties of the Welfare State* (1960), based mainly on her experiences in the East End of London, was reprinted several times. She tried to speak for a small minority, those dependent on State provision who still suffered great privation. This aim was one well in keeping with the Fabian tradition which was continued in the actions of CPAG. The minority she represented were the poor, not only those poor in terms of income but also 'in education, living space, opportunity and status'.

Her criticism was not only of social security provision but of the related services which it had been thought would form the complement to income-maintenance schemes. Again the Labour Party was criticised, with the Conservatives, for having over-estimated the extent to which working people had benefited from the reforms of the post-war Labour Government. She emphasised a theme shared by her colleagues in 'the rediscovery of poverty', that the neglect of poverty was partly due to the invisibility of the poor, who are today, 'scattered, isolated, not on view' (Harvey 1960: 31).

The emphasis in the Fabian publications and statements was on *information* and a reiteration of socialist values. Together these two, it was hoped, would be sufficient to remind the Labour movement of its priorities. The will to reform, together with practical proposals, would ensure the engineering of society towards egalitarianism and justice. The information and insights provided by these researchers and writers have been of immense value. In the 1950s there were virtually no government studies of poverty and social handicap and it was left to others, largely in the expanding universities and polytechnics, to provide the information. Now we are deluged with information. But has its *impact* increased? The information available is so complex that it takes many experts from different disciplines to unravel it, so that the debate is still confined to the elite of 'those who know'. The hope that information in itself would solve the problem of poverty has proved illusory. However, the sensitivity of social policy writers to what was happening enabled them to highlight the relevant issues. Indeed, it is remarkable how the issues of the 1950s anticipated the debates of the 1970s. For example, Richard Titmuss in 1960 wrote most perceptively about *The Irresponsible Society*:

It is one of the arguments of this essay that as the power of the insurance interests (in combination with other financial and commercial interests) continues to grow they will, whether they consciously welcome it or no, increasingly become the arbiters of welfare and amenity for larger sections of the community.

If one were looking for an epitaph for the Welfare State, it would be hard to find a better one than this. In drawing attention to the growing power of the insurance interests, Titmuss hit upon one of the keys to understanding social policy in post-war Britain. The insurance companies and pension funds are among the largest sources of new capital and their holdings are growing rapidly. Institutional investors exercise considerable influence over policy in companies where they are the single most important shareholder. In Britain, State pensions play second fiddle to employer-based pension schemes. When the pension scheme we have now was being discussed, persons and organisations for whom contracting out would be a source of profit campaigned successfully for favourable terms and, in proposing the abolition of earnings-related supplements in the 1980 budget, the Chancellor justified this by reference to the increase in occupational sick pay schemes.

Titmuss emphasised the 'need for strong, continuing and effective movements of protest and criticism. If they do not come from socialists and if they are not stated in terms of power, they will not come at all.' He was astute in pointing to opposing interests:

... a future historian, interested in the relationship between professional power and financial power, will have to take note of the several thousand statements made since 1945 attacking the 'immense and corrupting burden' of the 'welfare state' by insurance companies, banks, investment and hire purchase firms, the *British Medical Journal*, the Institute of Chartered Accountants, the British Employers' Federation, the Association of British Chambers of Commerce, the Institute of Directors, actuaries, judges and other professional men. Even as late as January 1960, the Chairman of Barclays Bank could say that the 'welfare state' had 'removed financial anxiety about illness and old age and had diminished in the ordinary man the sense of responsibility for his own future and that of his family'. (Titmuss 1960)

Through the Fabian Society, these academics attempted to influence the Labour movement to pay more attention to poverty and welfare. In the 1960s they became profoundly disillusioned by the shift in the orientation of the Labour Party towards 'economic growth' rather than 'equality' and 'social justice'. Their high hopes for the Labour Government were dashed. Initially, CPAG was set up simply as a pressure group aiming to redirect government policy in favour of low-income earners and the dependent and vulnerable members of the population. Their faith in the Labour Party was exemplified by their anticipation that their's would be a short-lived protest movement. As government actions belied their hopes, CPAG grew.

In 1965, 'a small group of sociologists and social workers decided to launch a campaign to bring the existence of family poverty to wider public notice and press for urgent government action to help those in need' (*Poverty* No 4 Autumn 1967: 26). The initial meeting was convened by the Social and Economic Affairs Committee of the Society of Friends and was addressed by Brian Abel-Smith. A group was formed and entitled the Advisory Council for the Alleviation of Poverty. Their aim was publicity, to put pressure on political leaders, particularly those in the Labour Party. 'So sunny was their confidence that this reasonable and desirable objective would be rapidly accomplished that it was twelve months before it even bothered to open a bank account.' (Rose and Jakubowicz 1978) The members were sure that the Labour Government would act to alleviate the problems of family poverty once they knew the facts. However, as no specific commitment could be wrung from the Labour Government, CPAG was formally constituted in February 1966. Its objective was to promote 'action for the relief, directly or indirectly, of poverty among children or families with children'. Tony Lynes, who had been Titmuss' research assistant and had worked briefly in the Ministry of Social Security, was appointed full-time secretary. Indeed, the poverty lobby at this time has been described as 'Tony Lynes on a bicycle!' In 1966, CPAG had 454 members. Ten years later there were 2,500.

The efforts of CPAG have been consistently directed towards the dissemination of information and the analysis, refutation of or comment on statements made by government officials, politicians or other pressure groups. An insistent and incessant flow of pamphlets, statements, articles in *New Society* and other journals, Press handouts and later books provided the 'public' with the 'facts' and the proposals of CPAG on how to remedy these social problems.

The officials of CPAG probably know as much or more about poverty and the workings of the present system of social security as any politician or civil servant. No budget is now drawn up without the Government receiving a 'memorandum' from CPAG reminding them of what they should do to improve the position of the poor and relatively deprived. Memos and submissions go to relevant House of Commons committees and advisory bodies. The stress has been largely on the irrationality of policy and practice, particularly with reference to the extension of means-tested benefits. Their main aim has been to promote the redistribution of income and universal social services.

Child Poverty Action Group became part of the fabric of British politics. The Chairman of the Supplementary Benefits Commission used to hold regular meetings with their representatives. Skilful use of the Press assures publicity for their demands. Personnel connected with the group have infiltrated government: Tony Lynes was an Advisor to the 1974 Labour Government and Frank Field was elected Labour MP for Birkenhead in 1979. Brian Abel-Smith was a Political Advisor to the Secretary of State for Social Services and David Piachaud was a member of the Prime Minister's 'Political Unit', when Labour was in power.

There has been demonstrably close contact between leaders of the poverty lobby and Labour Governments over two decades. How fair is it to conclude that this has had little effect on policy? Has 'academic debate become a substitute for organising the poor?' (Seyd 1976: 200). Opponents of this view could point out that there are those who attribute Labour's loss of the 1970 election to CPAG. Although this claim exaggerates the influence of their campaign, it was considerable. Arguing primarily to try to commit the Labour Party to raising family allowances in the next budget, CPAG produced evidence to show that 'the poor had got poorer under Labour'. Whatever the truth of this assertion, it was taken up by Tory campaigners and used against Labour. At the same time, it had the effect of committing the Conservative Party to increases in family allowances, a commitment which they later overturned, however, in favour of FIS, although it was at this time that the Conservative Government initiated proposals for child benefits. The memory of this attack is still painful to Labour MPs, and in 1979 the Labour Government was particularly careful to pre-empt such criticism by emphasising its new child benefit scheme and its pension plan. It would be wrong therefore to conclude that the influence of CPAG has been purely academic: the group has promoted wide *public* debate. The issues of poverty and inequality have been kept on the political agenda largely because of the barrage of information, analysis and comment that they have directed at the Government. They would admit that the part they have played in *organising* the poor has, however, been limited: they recognise that they are largely a middle-class organisation *for* the poor rather than *of* the poor.

A number of policies promoted by CPAG have eventually, after many years of campaigning, been accepted by Government. Their most notable success was that of child benefits. When Frank Field succeeded Tony Lynes in 1969 he made it clear that CPAG would continue to act as a pressure group for the poor and the major issue which he promoted was that of child benefits. He thought that an improvement in the situation of the poor could best be furthered by adding the 'elbow-power' of the middle classes to the campaign. Child Poverty Action Group began to develop into a 'family lobby' as well as being a 'poverty lobby'. But, in paying attention to the needs of families with children, the group did not neglect other poor people. The general orientation of their work has been to press for a real increase in the social security budget, to be financed through redistribution of the national income. Redistribution should take place from rich to poor; from the childless to those with children; from the younger to the older; from the consumers to low-paid producers; and from those in work to those out of work (Field 1978).

From the beginning CPAG concentrated on the needs of families with children, to redress the conception of poverty as a problem solely of old age. In 1978, for example, the majority of those people dependent on supplementary benefits were under pension age. The name chosen by the group was not simply a device to touch public conscience for in spite of the needs of children being supposedly recognised as more 'deserving' than others, thousands of children have continued to live in poverty. Other organisations such as Age Concern, the Disablement Income Group and The National Council. for One-Parent Families have been more specifically concerned with the needs of other groups. Later CPAG spawned another group, the Low Pay Unit, to concentrate on the issue of low pay, while CPAG would concentrate on the problems of children in poverty and of those dependent on supplementary benefits. The Low Pay Unit has produced its own statistical reports and commentaries on government statistics. It has a relatively more technical approach than other organisations. However, all these groups share a common purpose and are most effective when they can speak with one voice. For example, David Ennals the then Secretary of State for Social Services invited representatives from all 'client groups' to a seminar organised by the DHSS in 1977. The conclusion of the meeting was that the key priority should be an increase in family support. Even representatives of pensioners' organisations supported this demand, a united front that did much to commit the Labour Government to the introduction of improved child benefits.

The demand for higher family allowances was a prime one in CPAG's campaign from the beginning. In 1967, Patrick Gordon Walker, the Minister then responsible, said, 'By the end of the year we shall have dealt with family poverty' (16 July 1967 in Lincoln). Eight days later he announced 'an increase in family allowances . . . so ludicrously small that it can only have been intended as a sop to the Minister for Social Security, Miss Margaret Herbison, who had fought the Treasury for so long and with such little effect' (*Poverty* No 4 Autumn 1967). CPAG expressed their outrage:

Miss Herbison was asked to find the money for a solution to the problem of child poverty at the expense of the old, the sick and the unemployed, leaving the Chancellor to purloin the proceeds of a cut in tax allowance if he chose to do so. That she was right to resign in the circumstances is beyond question. The pity of it is that she did not feel free to reveal the whole disgraceful story thus laying the blame where it belongs – on Mr. Callaghan and the Board of Inland Revenue (ibid.)

This incident demonstrates CPAG's involvement in the political process. The discussions at the time were concerned with how to finance an increase in family allowances which would benefit poorer families while maintaining a universal service. Child Poverty Action Group had advocated, along the *The Times* and *The Economist*, experts and academics, the 'give and take' approach, later to be named 'clawback', an approach also favoured by Margaret Herbison. The pressure exerted by these groups supported her case in discussions with Ministers, particularly the Chancellor. However, their pressure was not sufficient, given the resistance of the Inland Revenue, who preferred to consider the tax system as separate from other areas of social policy. The Chancellor supported the Treasury and the Inland Revenue and Cabinet Ministers were divided, which was enough to ensure that the proposals were rejected. Part of the finance for the rise in family allowances at this time had to be found by raising the price of school meals and welfare milk.

The only option open to Margaret Herbison was to resign. Another role played by CPAG is also evidenced here – to be the channel for government leaks. Leaks may come from Cabinet Ministers or from civil servants but always 'the political barrel leaks from the top'. They may be used to warn the public of unpopular proposals and thus encourage opposition, or to minimise outrage by gradually letting the public know what is in store for them and thus get them used to the idea. Child Poverty Action Group has always had to transmit leaks in order to inspire opposition to government proposals and has had sometimes to modify its own more radical proposals to support its allies in the Cabinet. CPAG has been willing to make public the secret affairs of government, to expose issues and bring them to public attention through its own publications but, most importantly, through its contacts with the Press. Either through Press handouts or in the form of articles, short and long, CPAG is in constant correspondence with, in particular, *New Society*, *The Times*, the *Guardian* and the *New Statesman*.

One perennial problem for the campaign to increase child benefits has been the ambivalent attitude of the TUC. Trade unionists have always feared that the introduction or raising of family allowances would interfere with wage bargaining. A related problem, which would have to be dealt with in any successful incomes policy or evaluation of fair rates of pay, is that of whether wage levels should always be judged in terms of their adequacy for a *family man*. Without the balance being redressed, through either tax allowances or child benefits, this principle of a family wage acts to favour the childless man or woman and the two-income family. The trade unions' attitude to family allowances has fluctuated with their strength in wage negotiations. In 1941, for example, it was thought that the payment of allowances during the War would not materially handicap the unions in their fight to maintain and improve standards. In the autumn of 1942, after being consulted by Beveridge, the TUC Annual Conference declared its support for a national scheme of family allowance.

TUC interest waned after the War but revived in the 1960s, and, in 1964, they urged the Government to increase family allowances. Hugh Scanlon spoke in favour of increases in family allowances in 1968. As part of the 'social contract', they promoted increases in child benefit. Support from the leaders of the Labour movement (whatever was being said in the Labour Clubs in Leeds) helped CPAG's campaign. However, the 1974 Labour administration was reluctant to increase family allowances and implement its child benefit scheme because they were deemed unpopular in public opinion and because it was felt there would be a male backlash about redistributing money from husbands to wives. David Ennals reported to his colleagues in Cabinet, in an effort to prevent their vetoing this policy, that families with children were then getting substantially less financial support than the Conservative Government provided in 1970, 1971 and 1972 and less than under Labour in the late 1960s. This report was leaked spectacularly to the Press, a leak facilitated by the close contacts which had been built up among the political elite by the poverty lobby and one which demonstrates their willingness to sail close to the wind on occasions. The leak had two effects. The Government decided to introduce child benefits after all, but phasing them in over a period of time, and an additional payment of £300 million was made.

As developed by Frank Field, the campaign for increased child benefits promoted the interests of all families, not just those of the poor. Part of the earlier emphasis on the need for higher child benefits had been linked to a campaign to help the low-paid: 'the low wage earner and his family who, because those in full-time work cannot claim supplementary benefit, could not be brought up to the minimum level, and who were kept in poverty by the 'wage-stop' when the father was out of work' (*Poverty* No 7 Summer 1968). By 1976 these two issues had been affected by the introduction of FIS and the abolition of the 'wage-stop'. Although not ideal, it was unrealistic to expect further action from the Chancellor or the DHSS. It was tactically relevant, therefore, to focus on the needs of the low-paid in incomes policy, the problem of the impact of inflation on tax thresholds and to press for further increases in child benefits. Given the resistance in public opinion to increasing child benefit, since it was thought to be a gain for the profligate poor, one way to alter this opinion was to emphasise the value of child benefits to families as a whole as an addition which helped those with the greatest domestic responsibilities. Particularly in a period of wage restraint, additional income in the form of child benefits would be generally welcomed by the middle class and more affluent working class as much as by poor families. Interestingly, in 1979, following the departure of Frank Field and after incomes policy had been discarded, Ruth Lister, the new Director of CPAG said the Group should again give more emphasis to the 'poorest families'.

This switch of emphasis reflects also the change of government. The tactics of a pressure group vary with the colour of the Government. The link between poverty and inequality was promoted strongly by CPAG and the Low Pay Unit while Labour was in power. With the election of a Government led by one who believes that 'the fact about economic inequality (as opposed to the myth) is that the rich are getting poorer and the poor are getting richer' (Thatcher 1977) and with the cuts in public expenditure, the priority has quite rightly again become that of protecting the interests of the very weak.

A further issue emphasised by CPAG has been the underestimation of the costs of raising children. First publicised by Margaret Wynn in her book, *Family Policy* (1970), this point has been taken up increasingly in recent years. The undervaluing of the costs involved leads to inadequate provision for children in supplementary benefit rates.

In the campaign for increased child benefit and more concern for the needs of families, CPAG has acted not only for two-parent families. One-parent families have a similar interest in these demands. Here, CPAG has cooperated with the National Council for One-Parent Families and its sister organisation, Gingerbread. The campaign involved pressure to extend family allowances to the first child and later to see additions being made to these rates for the unsupported single parent.

These pressure groups act as watch-dogs on the activities of Governments on behalf of their clients or members. They remind Governments of their responsibilities and their promises, comment on developments in policy and practice and propose solutions. They have been aided in this by the enormous increase in information that is now provided by government. It could even be said that it was precisely this increase in information that produced the need for pressure groups which would digest, analyse, simplify and disseminate the information to a wider audience. Each has certainly led to an increase in the activity of the other. In the 1950s there were few government investigations. One major success for the Fabians was to encourage government to initiate a series of studies relevant to poverty and welfare. One important investigation was that of *Circumstances of Families* (1966). Another was that of the Committee of One-Parent Families. This, the *Finer Report* (1974) proposed a new social security benefit for one-parent families, the guaranteed maintenance allowance (GMA), to replace maintenance payments and remove these parents and children from dependence on supplementary benefits. In spite of the elegance of its proposals and the awareness of need, the Finer Report has now been buried and it is most unlikely that it will be implemented in the forseeable future. Any proposal which involves extra cost seems doomed to failure in the present climate. In addition, the proposal for GMA was based on the hope that the taxation and social security systems would be more closely coordinated in future. Labour's income guarantee and the Conservatives' negative income tax scheme (much criticised by CPAG) were based on the assumption that such a plan was feasible. As the difficulties of this coordination have been uncovered, its realisation has tended to be postponed, although not indefinitely. It is likely that, following computerization in the 1980s, such schemes may then become practicable.

The role played by international pressure in the reforms of the

1940s should be recalled. The ideas of the New Deal and the apparent benefits of the Russian system encouraged the notion of the Welfare State in Britain, not least as an alternative to the competing claims of the Soviet Union and Nazi Germany. In recent years, international pressure has been generally viewed as unfavourable to social reform. The influence of the IMF has been seen as particularly significant. In 1976, it insisted on strict policies to cut public expenditure. However, more progressive currents are also present. In the switch to earnings-related pensions and benefits in the 1960s and the encouragement of occupational pensions, comparative studies and the policies of other western countries were influential. In making many of these changes the UK was falling into line with other EEC countries. The aim to encourage labour mobility within the EEC directly fosters the standardization of social security arrangements. Such influence works through the civil service and affects recommendations made by departments to Ministers.

In the campaign for increased child benefits, international comparisons supported the case. Particularly during the seventies, many countries switched their system of financing benefits from tax allowances to cash transfers. This change occurred in Britain in 1977 but had already been carried out in Australia, Canada, Denmark, West Germany, Italy and New Zealand. Here, then, the initiative came from changes in tax arrangements and these had an impact on social security. Compulsory joint taxation of husband and wife had been phased out in nearly all countries and, with progressive rates of taxation and an increase in two-income families, the tendency to opt for the more advantageous individual taxation increased. It was argued that this gain to high-income units could be offset by payment of child benefit, a gain to the lower-paid. If this factor did play a part, it reflects the influence of fair-minded public officials. The source of this 'fair-mindedness', an interest in equity and parity, lies in the institutionalization of professional ethics and departmental responsibilities in a predominantly social democratic milieu.

CPAG's Campaign on child benefits could be said to have had some effect. Without their efforts, things might have been a good deal worse. In November 1978, child benefit rose from £2.30 to £3, then to £4 in April 1979, with an extra £2 for one-parent families, and to £4.75 in November 1980. Child benefits seemed to be moving towards an acceptable level. The raising of child benefits proved to be more popular than Labour had anticipated, so much so that they went into the next election campaigning as the party which cared about the family, with posters showing a genial Jim Callaghan presiding over a large family gathering. But this success proved short-lived. The abolition of child tax allowances brought low-paid families into the tax net, a situation made worse by the abolition of the lower 25 per cent rate of income tax in 1980. The situation could be alleviated by the raising of tax thresholds but it is one which leaves these families ever vulnerable to the effects of inflation. The combination of the failure to index child benefits, rising inflation and cuts in some means-tested benefits for the low-paid (such as school meals, help with transport and heating) has had the effect of reversing any gains to the lower-paid achieved in the seventies. Both the poverty lobby and the family lobby are back where they started twenty years ago. Child benefits in 1980 have almost the same value as family allowances in 1955. The campaign for child benefits at an acceptable level and protection of the relative and absolute position of the poor has to begin all over again.

A different kind of political force are those which aim to be organisations *of* the poor rather than *for* the poor. These are the Claimants Unions. They originated in the activities of Joe Kenyon, a Yorkshire ex-miner, and separately in those, of a group of socialist students in Birmingham in 1968. By 1971, there were 88 autonomous unions, loosely joined as the National Federation of Claimants Unions. Generally, the members of these unions have defended their integrity vehemently against infiltration by restricting their membership to past and present claimants. This is an important policy since far-left groups have often infiltrated similar associations, in so doing generally leading to their collapse. Welfare rights were especially well promoted by telling claimants not only *what* their rights were but also *how* to get them. With the vast expansion in the seventies in the use of discretionary powers in granting supplementary benefits there was a parallel increase in the occurrence of variation and anomalies both between and within local areas. Local Claimants Unions exposed these disparities and also represented their members at tribunals and appeals.

Claimants Unions have lost ground recently, partly due to the recession, but the pressure placed on DHSS local offices by the increasing volume of work in dealing with the claims of the poor for assistance has led to a situation of near breakdown in the existing machinery. Whether deliberately through CPAG and the Claimants Unions, or less deliberately but no less effectively by individual claimants themselves, the exercise of claiming and the demand for fair treatment bring the influence of poor people themselves directly to bear. Their presence, their need and demand for assistance increasingly disrupt the official procedures, which cannot cope with the changed situation. In the inter-war years and in the 1940s, this kind of pressure led to change. Similarly, in recent years the pressure placed on machinery designed to deal with a problem which has altered in size and shape is leading to changes in the administration of social security. It was especially the changing composition of claimants which had an immediate effect – they are now less likely to be the old and tired and more likely to be parents with children who are more vociferous and active in pushing their claims. But it should not be forgotten that the *direction* of such changes is influenced by the wider political milieu. It is in affecting attitudes at this level, in suggesting policies and criticising proposals, that those acting *for* the poor can make their contribution.

Strategies of disruption have also been pursued by unions representing the low-paid, particularly the public sector unions. Those who condemn their tactics should remember that for the poor and powerless, disruption is the one effective weapon they have. Claims for a minimum wage, for an improvement in the relative position of the low-paid, are of equal importance in the drive to improve the lot of the poor.

These political forces directly representing the poor are supported by, if not exactly a cast of thousands, a larger number of organisations. On specific issues these will add their weight to the campaign. Closest are those organisations which represent other clients of the Welfare State like Shelter, Age Concern, Disablement Income Group (DIG), National Council for One Parent Families (NCOPF), and Campaign for the Single Homeless (CHAR). In the short term, these organisations exert pressure on ministers and civil servants. In the longer term they build up links with political parties and associations.

An important force acting in the interests of the poor has been created by the extension of the Welfare State itself. Those employed in the public sector have a direct and immediate interest in maintaining these institutions. Those employed in the expanding 'caring professions' and in the lower levels of the civil and public services are often of working-class origin themselves. They might in earlier times have formed part of the leadership of the Labour movement. The codes of practice built into the institutions of the Welfare State can also be used to protect the interests of the poor, as was in essence the hope of Fabian socialism. Although not inevitably evolving along the road of social progress, these institutions and the men and women who work within them can provide a base from which the goal of welfare can be pursued.

One institution which exemplifies this point is the SBC. The establishment of the SBC as an independent agency within the DHSS added an important source of pressure on behalf of the poor. The Commission's main function was to ensure that people got the supplementary benefit to which they were entitled. The Supplementary Benefit Act provided that those whose resources were insufficient to meet their requirements were entitled to the rates of benefit laid down by Parliament each year and also gave the Commission wide powers to make special provision in particular cases. The massive increase in discretionary payments in the seventies largely resulted from the vigorous implementation of these powers. The position of the Chairman of the SBC was a powerful one that could be utilised in the interests of the clients of the DHSS, given commitment and dynamism. The appointment of David Donnison to this position in 1974 continued the LSE and academic connection. Donnison had been Professor of Social Administration at LSE from 1961 to 1969. He was Director of the Centre for Environmental Studies from 1969 to 1975. From 1973, he was Deputy Chairman of the Commission. Other members of the Commission represented experts, academics, trade unions, local authority social service departments, political parties and those with a record of public service. When Donnison was appointed the Secretary of State said he intended '. . . to make greater use of the Commission as an advisory body in referring issues to them for advice . . . and in looking to them for ideas on research in their field and on priorities for development of policies as and when resources permitted and more generally for promotion of studies of future development of social policies.' (*Hansard* 2 May 1975, vol. 891 Col. 262) This power was used extensively. An indication of the open and responsive tone of Donnison's administration was the publication in 1975 of the first *Annual Report* of the Supplementary Benefits Commission. Through the *Annual Reports* important and useful information was provided and critical issues highlighted. Both in public and within the civil service, the SBC exercised an independent voice. In general, it supported the liberal reforms advocated by CPAG and experts in social administration. For example, in 1976, SBC supported the case for improved child benefit. This voice, together with that of the political parties, trade unions and pressure groups,

The politics of poverty

helped to promote the changes which occurred in 1978. The Supplementary Benefits Commission was able to point out trends in social security, such as the increase in long-term unemployment, and give information on the rates of take-up of means-tested allowances and the increasing use of discretionary payments. In this way it could contribute to attempts at rational planning of social policy. The SBC was also responsive to appeals from pressure groups: for example, concern was expressed by welfare rights workers at the secrecy surrounding decisions about supplementary benefit payments. Pressure was put on the SBC to publish the 'A' code, a code of guidance issued to civil servants at local social security offices (employed incidentally by the DHSS not by SBC). In response to this pressure, the Supplementary Benefits Handbook was published. This was a guide to claimants' rights first published in 1970 and revised in later editions. It did not include all the codes of practice sent to local offices and was still, therefore, open to criticism. But it did help claimants and welfare rights workers. In 1974, the secret 'A' codes were leaked to the press and this again revived the debate. It was pressures like these for an extension of welfare rights which contributed directly to the setting up in September 1976 of the review of supplementary benefit procedures (Social Assistance).

In all this, the significance of having access to information and being able to understand and interpret technical or obscure information is very clear. Research work plays a part here. There are now about 242 social scientists working in central government as specialists. Forty-seven are employed in the Department of the Environment, 40 in the Office of Population Censuses and Surveys (OPCS), 32 at the Home Office but only 22 in the DHSS. Research commissioned by the SBC focused on issues relevant to the aim of ensuring that those entitled to supplementary benefit received it. Other research has been commissioned by the DHSS. This is generally conducted by the staff of universities. An important growth has been that of research officers and advisers within government. Some have seen these political and policy advisers as a 'grave constitutional threat or political mafia'. The label 'special adviser' was coined in 1974 to describe the growing collection of advisers, aides and hangers-on that Conservative and Labour Ministers brought with them or acquired in office. But their impact has in fact been very limited. Some have introduced new perspectives and encouraged rational planning. Some have fed in new ideas and research results. Yet, given the power of the civil service 'in this environment, it would have been absurd to expect a few dozen special advisers, however exceptional, to effect a transformation and they have not done so' (*New Society* 22 June 1978). In fact it was the frustration felt by these special advisers which produced some of the more dramatic of the leaks of classified information in the seventies. The 8,000 senior civil servants in Whitehall provide a more than adequate counterweight to their zeal. In Whitehall, it is said, it is the ministry rather than the minister which matters, the career civil servants rather than the ambitions of each fleeting group of politicians. But 'it is wrong to see the civil service simply as an *obstructive* force. The departments, like the Treasury, have positive policies to press upon Ministers. By the nature of their work, civil servants have a belief in state action. Paternalism and centralism still rule in Whitehall.' (*New Society* 10 May 1979)

Contacts between research workers in government and university researchers are close and fostered by conferences and seminars. Research workers see themselves as separate from other civil servants. They follow a different career pattern and speak with an independent voice. They emphasise the perspective of their profession or discipline and attempt to further rational planning rather than departmental or political interests. The emphasis on Government-commissioned research, promoted by the Rothschild Report, aims to focus research on socially relevant questions although some have seen it as a threat to academic freedom. University researchers receiving grants from DHSS, for example, are limited in their freedom to publish their findings. They have to guard against unhelpful interference in the research process.

Indeed, research workers have wondered how much notice is taken of their results in practice. They complain that the lack of interest in the results 'is discouraging and leaves one in doubt as to the value of the work to the sponsors' (Olive Stevenson and Michael J. Hill, DHSS 1977a: 73). With reference to descriptive and analytic work, rather than results presented solely in quantitative terms, the same researchers comment, 'we are left with the feeling that our sponsors do not value this type of research material or that it is not accepted that the researchers might have a part to play in policy once "the goods" are delivered' (ibid.). To some extent the growth of research in recent years has had a similar function to that of Royal Commissions in the past. That it is being carried out and has been sponsored by government can be used as a device to demonstrate that the Government is aware of the issue and is doing something about it. Critics can be shown that the Government is responsive and concerned. The Government is defended against attack from its political opponents. It can also be used as a delaying tactic: the Government, both politicians and civil servants, need not and should not act until the results of research are known. It is politically helpful that so much academic research often takes an inordinate time to complete and even longer to publish. The lack of interest of government in the results, so disappointing to the researchers, reflects the fact that by the time their reports are submitted, the issue is dead or decisions have already been taken, influenced not by 'rational' considerations, but rather by power politics. To counter such criticism, research grants have more recently been tied to small-scale social experiments or action-research programmes. Government can then be seen to be sponsoring not only study but action. The limited nature of these programmes, however, in time and space, contrasts with the proposals for reform in the system as a whole generally advocated by those pressing for improvements.

Professionals employed by government as research officers and advisers complain that, while they had hoped to become more immediately involved in policy-making, to exert an influence from within, their time is actually spent providing information for their departmental heads. These heads seem, however, to make decisions without reference to the details they provide. They are used mainly to service the department, to provide answers to Parliamentary questions, or to counter the criticisms of outside pressure groups. They offer a technical service and they try to do this with integrity, but their attention is directed to issues raised by others. They are not allowed to focus on the issues which they consider to be important.

The Supplementary Benefits Commission, however, did not succumb to such pressures. This was largely because of its status and proximity to the elite of decision-makers. It was able to promote the interests of the poor and powerless. The independence of the SBC was important and demonstrated how institutional reform can benefit specific groups in the community. However, such reform should never be taken for granted nor assumed to be permanent for the SBC was abolished on November 24 1980. Thus the cause of the poor suffered a major reverse. It is ironic that one benefit of separate services is that the otherwise fragmented and disorganised poor can be represented in the authority structure by those who work with and for them.

Another example of government-initiated reform which raised the same issues even more starkly was that of the Community Development Projects (CDPs) of the late 1960s. Joan Higgins has condemned the higher civil servants responsible, with their bizarre jumble of unjustified assumptions about the characteristics of the poor. They failed to coordinate action. Their loyalty was to departmental expansion rather than to the deprived. The beneficiaries were academics and universities and those local authorities proficient in grantmanship, not necessarily those in the greatest need (Higgins 1978). Community Development Projects were clearly intended as a device to counter the criticisms of political opponents, who came not only from the Left, that not enough was being done to alleviate poverty and distress. One important critic of the Right was Enoch Powell who, in a famous speech in spring 1968 at Birmingham, foretold 'rivers of blood'.

These ventures, however, did not work entirely against the interests of the poor. Some of those who worked on those projects contributed to the stream of information which kept the issue of poverty alive (North Tyneside CDP 1978). This should not be underestimated, although it is of course the minimum required for social reform. Activists in these projects, following (like the welfare rights campaigners) their American counterparts, hoped to strengthen local political institutions, especially tenants' and residents' groups. What these movements exposed was the conspicuous failure of the Labour Party to represent the interests of the disadvantaged at the local level. The dearth of active local representation by Labour has been evident since the 1960s, especially in the inner city areas (Hindess 1971). The failure of the Labour Party, particularly the drying up of its grass roots at the local level has been a major force acting against the interests of the poor. This is especially important since the Labour Party traditionally represented these sections and still claims to do so.

Of crucial importance to the tactics employed by pressure groups, with their emphasis on informing and publicizing, is the existence of a free press and of journals and newspapers prepared to publish leaks and to give prominence to their articles, reports and statements. The lack of a radical newspaper is notable in Britain, but the *Guardian* and *New Society* play an important role in informing their liberal middle-class readers, especially the 'low' intellectuals, professionals and civil servants. Additionally, plays and documentaries like *Cathy Come Home, Edna The Inebriate Woman* and, most impressive of all, *The Spongers* exerted influence on public opinion. *New Society* has been very important and its history demonstrates that concern for social reform is not necessarily linked with the Labour Party. Timothy Raison, now a Minister of State at the Home Office in Mrs Thatcher's government, was the first Editor of *New Society*, a sister publication to *New Scientist*, devoted to the social sciences. The first issue of *New Society* appeared on 4 October 1962 and many of its subscribers are social workers or social administrators. It is interesting that this development occurred in the same year as the establishment of the Social Science Research Council (SSRC), giving the official seal of approval to social studies. The expansion of social sciences in higher education has not in itself led to the promotion of progressive or radical ideas in spite of the scares of Julius Gould, Professor of Sociology at Nottingham University, and his colleagues. The activities of those who choose to study problems of policy have often been sneered at as non-scientific, a-theoretical or empiricist, both by Marxist and Conservative academics incidentally. This echoes the snobbery encountered by Titmuss. After his appointment to a chair at LSE, he found that there were some who insisted on pretending to think he was Professor of Midwifery, rather than of Social Administration.

Through the expansion of the social sciences, a vast amount of new knowledge relevant to social problems has been accumulated. *New Society* has been important in selecting from this the ideas and results of relevance to policy and practice, and publishing these in a readable and undistorted form, thereby widening the audience for this knowledge.

FORCES WORKING AGAINST THE POOR

The failure of the Labour Party is all the more important given the weight of the forces acting against the interests of the poor. When these are considered, the actions of CPAG can be compared to the efforts of the Health Education Council in the battle with the tobacco, alcohol and advertising industries. In the construction of public opinion, the role of the popular and Right-wing Press is of immense significance.

'Scrounging' means cadging other people's left-overs or picking things up illicitly. Dislike of scrounging is in itself not new. But in the 1970s there was increasing reference to scrounging or sponging in connection with welfare payments. This coincided with a change in the composition of claimants. Where in the 1950s and 1960s about half of all old-age pensioners were forced to claim supplementary benefits, at the beginning of the 1980s this proportion was down to one-fifth, as a result of the attention given to the problem of old-age pensions. However, in 1980 about half of all single-parent families were dependent on supplementary benefits, as were an increasing proportion of the unemployed. As more claimants came to be people of working age and their families, the label 'scrounger' was applied more often and public indignation whipped up against them.

The campaign of scrounger-bashing reached its height in 1976. It began with an allegation by a Conservative MP, Iain Sproat, that only half of those receiving unemployment benefit were really looking for work. It happened that at this time a man nicknamed 'King Fiddler', Derek Deevey, was convicted of having drawn £36,000 in benefit using 41 aliases. This was certainly a newsworthy item – but it was also used as a peg around which to hang a series of attacks on 'professional job-dodgers', men between the ages of 18 and 36 who were 'idle to the backbone and twice as devious'. The rising rate of unemployment had forced supplementary benefit officers to limit the application of the four-week rule. This rule, introduced in 1968 as part of a series of disciplinary measures particularly directed at the low-paid and unskilled, stipulated that any single, unskilled man under the age of 45 would be granted SB for only four weeks. The rule should operate only under certain conditions – if unskilled jobs are available in the locality; if the claimant is not suffering from any serious physical disability and has shown no signs of mental disorder; or if the claimant is unskilled. It was described as a scandal by Molly Meacher in her book *Scrounging on the Welfare* (1974). It is worth noting that there are now suggestions that this rule will be applied with more vigour in future.

After the uprating of benefits in November 1976, the attacks strengthened, with increased emphasis on the difference between incomes in and out of work. *The Times* called for the reintroduction of the wage-stop (abolished in 1974 by Labour after years of campaigning by pressure groups). The real problem of low wages and the reduction in tax thresholds was discussed much less than that of benefits being too generous. Robert Adley, another Conservative MP, claimed that ordinary people were sick and tired of seeing their taxes squandered on people who would not know what a day's work looked like if it stared them in the face. Such statements were quoted widely in the Press and contributed to a hardening of attitudes towards the poor.

David Donnison explained this reaction as occurring because

people had lost faith in economic growth and were compelled to recognise that any help given to poorer people must be paid for by real reductions in their own living standards.

An important study of this phenomenon has been carried out by Peter Golding and Sue Middleton (1978), who point out that 1976 was a year in which public expenditure cuts were introduced, at the same time as the real value of wages was actually declining. Golding and Middleton analysed all welfare and social security news stories on TV news, in the national Press, and in the local Press and radio in two cities. 'No fewer than 30.8 per cent of all stories dealt in some way with social security abuse.' A recurrent theme was a conspiracy thesis: that the very lack of concrete evidence of widespread abuse only proved the expertise, deviousness and organisation of the culprits. Iain Sproat MP, for instance, believed the known numbers must be only the tip of a vast iceberg (Daily Express 14 July 1976). A *Daily Express* editorial on 18 December 1977 commented on the results of an investigation which showed welfare abuse to be confined to a very small number: 'It is the official figure based upon frauds which have been found out. Nobody knows how much larger the figure would be if we could take into account the undiscovered fiddlers and thieves.' The *Daily Mirror* also took up the theme of large numbers referring to 'Britain's army of dole-queue swindlers' (quoted in Golding and Middleton 1978).

Not only the tabloid Press purveys these myths. The *Daily Telegraph* continued its long tradition of attacking the Welfare State, insisting in September 1976 that 'supplementary benefit should be what it used to be known as in a less euphemistic era: assistance. It should be a safety net, strictly for emergencies, not a featherbed for every hard luck case around.'

Such featherbedding was thought to allow those on supplementary benefit to take expensive Spanish holidays. Some made do, it seemed, with holidays in Britain: an article in the *Daily Mail* (13 July 1977) entitled 'Scroungers by the Sea' described the seaside social security offices which 'are thick with subsidised cigarette smoke, the smell of alcohol paid for by the state and the smugly tanned faces of the leeches feeding off the hardworking, ordinary, silent majority'. Such moral outrage, Golding and Middleton perceptively point out, serves the purpose of 'dissolving the distinction between economic and moral inadequacy'.

This kind of publicity encourages unsympathetic attitudes to the poor, while in the poor themselves it adds to the feelings of rejection, stigma and reluctance to claim means-tested benefits. Child

Poverty Action Group emphasised the double morality of a public which is outraged by welfare abuse but unconcerned about tax evasion and the underpayment of minimum wages. £36 million is paid out *daily* in social security benefits: in one *year* only £3.2 million was fraudulently claimed. It should be remembered, however, that in 1976, £27 million was recovered from detected fraud and evasion of taxes. Is this too the tip of the iceberg? In 1980, while social security inspectors were being increased, the number of Inland Revenue staff engaged on detecting income tax evasion was actually reduced.

The Supplementary Benefits Commission and Government Ministers tried to counter these allegations. The Labour Government's first response in July 1976, however, implied tacit agreement with the reports. Stan Orme announced the introduction of a number of new measures in September 1976, including surprise visits to the homes of some claimants. These measures were not in fact new but were given prominence to placate public opinion. More usefully, the DHSS carried out investigations into the cases of alleged fraud submitted by Iain Sproat MP. The first 196 cases analysed were found to contain only 17 cases of fraud, 9 of which were already under investigation. These results were published in February 1977 and they served to vindicate the Department against the charge of laxity. By June 1977 a total of 441 cases had been examined and fresh evidence of fraud had been uncovered in only 22. The House of Commons took note of these findings. The extreme views of Sproat had to give way to more moderate opinion within the Conservative Party, but they had little effect on public opinion since they went largely unreported in those newspapers which had played such a prominent part in the attack.

David Donnison consistently rebutted these allegations, with some effect within the elite. However, the number of special investigators employed by the DHSS has increased from 22 in 1955 to 428 in 1978, and to 1,000 in 1980. 'Fraud Awareness Packages' were circulated first in 1977 and again in 1979 to local offices. The emphasis given to fraud detection in itself fosters in the minds of staff at local offices the suspicion that claimants are devious liars and affects relationships between claimants and staff adversely. These Press reports increase public hostility to the poor. We have already noted that the attitudes of the British public to the poor are extremely harsh when compared with the attitudes of people in other EEC countries. Margaret Morris found similarly hostile attitudes in her survey and these seemed to be increasing: 'People perceived to be least in need of help included "lazy students", "selfish layabouts", "people scrounging on unemployment benefits", "malingerers", "frauds", and "people who have brought trouble upon themselves".'(Morris 1978)

It would be quite wrong to indict the whole of the Conservative Party for these attitudes, in spite of the part played by some Conservative MPs. Patrick Jenkin commented in 1977,

I warmly endorse the view that rather than raise hysterical dust about the small minority that abuse the system, the real need is to concentrate on reform of the system itself. In the recent uprating, not a single pensioner was lifted off supplementary benefit; there was no reduction of means-testing; there was no easing of the poverty trap; and nobody was given a bigger incentive to work. These aims will only be achieved by going over to a tax credits scheme. Conservatives have recently completed a major policy project on this subject with a view to phasing in such a scheme as soon as possible ... Tax credits hold the field as the only viable way ahead. (Letter to *New Society* November 1977)

These views were, however, expressed while in Opposition. There are no signs yet (in 1981) that progressive, compassionate or family-centred policies will be carried out by the Conservative Government. There is, however, some consistency between Conservative statements in Opposition and in Government. Pensioners' benefits have been raised, but in line with price rises rather than earnings. There has been a reduction in means-testing, but by the simple expedient of abolishing a large number of means-tested benefits. The poverty trap has been eased, not by raising the incomes of the low-paid, but by cutting the standard of living of the unemployed. Hunger and cold may well turn out to be the biggest incentive to work.

Reform of the social security system is now going ahead. The trend towards selectivism, reductions in public expenditure, an economy in recession, resistance to redistribution of income, rising unemployment and hostility towards the poor form the context within which decisions about reform will be taken. A negative income tax scheme in itself is a neutral proposition. What matters are the rates of payment and the cut-off points. Such schemes accord well with the monetarist ideas now dominant. The guru of monetarists is the economist and Nobel prize-winner, Milton Friedman, whose view of Britain's social machinery is that

it does not do what its well-meaning proponents intended. What it does is to take from some poor to give to the other poor or even to the middle classes. Also the welfare state has been a road to higher incomes and more security for the people who administer it and they are the main obstacles to eliminating it. There is no reason why you could not substitute voucher schemes or negative income tax for much of your present welfare programme. You could do it at less cost and with greater benefit to the people who really need help. (*The Times* 13 September 1976: 7)

The interests of the poor and other clients of the Welfare State and those employed in the public sector clearly coincide when drastic cuts in provision are instigated; but it should be noted that those employed in the Welfare State, like members of the Labour Party, are not necessarily motivated by high ideals of social justice. Friedman's view was shared by Titmuss years earlier, when he pointed out the danger that the Welfare State might serve the interests of the comfortable members of the so-called caring professions more than those of their clients.

It is striking that new solutions to the problems of poverty and welfare have come from the Right, from Friedman, the Institute of Economic Affairs (IEA) and the Conservative Party. These solutions are not of course *new*. They have their origins in the social arrangements and ideas which prevailed before the advent of the mixed economy and the Welfare State.

The connection between the IEA and the Conservative Party is not direct, in spite of the peerage awarded to Ralph Harris in Margaret Thatcher's first Honours List. The two men central to IEA, Ralph Harris and Arthur Seldon, have not been firm supporters of the Conservative Party. They claim to have had as many contacts with members of the Labour Party as with the Conservative. Their aim has been to promote free-market ideas, especially among economists. IEA was launched in January 1957. Harris and Seldon have taken up Hayek's attack on collectivism. They do not agree that their policies attack the poor but say that their policies, by promoting economic growth, would increase the prosperity of the working class. Their proposals would emancipate the poor, by giving them freedom of choice, freedom from the paternalism and monopolies of the State. Financial support for IEA came originally from Anthony Fisher of Buxted Chickens, a pioneer of factory farming. The Institute of Economic Affairs now receives support from big companies like ICI, Unilever, Shell, Lucas, Courtaulds and Guest, Keen and Nettlefold, although retaining its independence, and essentially provides the counter-attack to the Fabians. Its advisory council consists of academics and economists like Colin Clark, Alan Peacock, Jack Wiseman and A.R. Prest. With the dearth of ideas among politicians and the general disillusionment with parties, support has grown for their proposals that cash should count, that money should talk. Individuals know best how to spend the money they themselves earn through their work. Decisions about goods and services and about priorities should be made by each individual exercising his own freedom of choice in the economic market.

What IEA has done is question the operation of the welfare system and propose solutions for reform which have proved attractive because of the lack of alternatives. The results of surveys carried out by IEA show the growing resistance to taxation. Between the sixties and late seventies, the proportion willing to pay more for an improved health service fell from 41 per cent to 20 per cent and for improved education from 51 per cent to 15 per cent. Only a small and declining minority are prepared to pay for further improvement (Harris and Seldon 1979). There is little doubt that such resistance is present and growing. The proposals made by IEA are open to greater doubt, however, as are some of its wilder conclusions, for instance that 'the Welfare State has gradually changed from the expression of compassion to an instrument of political repression unequalled in British history and in other western industrialised countries' (op. cit.: 204).

Another counterweight to Fabian thinking which has influenced the Conservative Party (and may have influenced civil servants if they dutifully took note of the reading lists distributed by Sir Keith Joseph on assuming office) is the Centre for Policy Studies, founded by Sir Keith in 1974, whose ideas of economic liberalism aim to sweep away the liberal conservatism of the post-war era, principally to roll back the frontiers of the State and maintain or increase inequality. Conservatives argue, of course, that there is no connection between poverty and inequality. The pursuit of equality has not aided the poor but has had as its main motivation the politics of envy. 'The destruction of incentive condemns the economy to stagnation and the poor to hopeless penury.' (Lawson 1979)

CONCLUSION

As Titmuss noted in his lecture on 'The Irresponsible Society' (1960), the initiative in welfare has been taken by the pension funds, with the cooperation of employers and trade unions. In developing occupational pension schemes, sickness schemes, and other fringe benefits, they have undermined the national social security system. The most important political forces affecting the poor have not been directly concerned with them. In fact, they have conspicuously ignored them. The principle of collective provision with its egalitarian aspirations has been effectively destroyed by these developments. The traditional supporters of the poor, the Fabians and the liberal middle classes, Christians, voluntary organisations and charitable foundations, have continued to defend their interests and have been aided in recent years by new groups, particularly sections within the institutions of the Welfare State itself, public sector employees and the growing trades of social work and social science. The disruption caused to the machinery of administration by the actions of Claimants Unions and welfare rights workers focused attention on the poor in ways that these organisations for the poor could never do. Pressure groups devoted to their cause expanded as the Labour Party, especially in the 1960s, effectively withdrew its commitment. Aided by the liberal Press, they fought long and hard on specific issues, with one or two successes, particularly in the seventies when they won the support of the Labour Party and Trade Unions. But the forces acting against the interests of the poor, especially sections of the popular Press and the growing resistance to increased taxation, seem to write out any possibility of an improvement in the lot of the poor in the near future. Improvement can only be achieved through a redistribution of resources, through policies raising the wages of the low-paid and through increased benefits. And no section of society is ready to accept that wholeheartedly. The most significant force acting against the poor is the resistance of entrenched interests to a reduction in their share of the goods and services available. No section, it seems, is willing to accept a cut in its share in order to benefit the poor. Reallocation would have to be in the face of not only unwillingness but also determined opposition. Is it possible to overcome such opposition?

Part three
WHAT SHOULD BE DONE?

Chapter eight
THE AGENDA FOR REFORM

The effects of the immunisation of class conflict inherent in the consensus politics of the post-war years were, as Habermas noted:

a) disparate wage development and/or a sharpening of wage disputes in the public service sector; b) permanent inflation with corresponding temporary redistribution of income to the disadvantage of unorganised workers and other marginal groups; c) permanent crisis in government finances, together with public poverty (that is, impoverishment of public transportation, education, housing and health care); and d) an inadequate adjustment of disproportional economic developments, sectoral (agriculture) as well as regional (marginal areas). (Habermas 1976:38)

In the coming years, the poor will continue to be vulnerable to attack, as Government searches for ways of cutting public expenditure without losing the votes of its key supporters. The major priority must be, therefore, to maintain the standard of living of the poor and the poorest and to preserve the benefits and services that have been built up.

Indexing of social security benefits, the extension of the long-term rate to the unemployed and an improvement in the children's rate of supplementary benefit are priorities as far as claimants are concerned. Recently, the attack on the poor has been directed mainly at the working poor. The best way to protect them would be to raise the value of child benefits and index these to prices and to raise tax thresholds. Housing and fuel subsidies are needed to protect both claimants and the low-paid with families.

Protection of services and the pursuit of these policies will have to be given priority in the immediate future, and support for these policies will need to be attracted from centre politicians and Tory paternalists. The help of these sections of the Conservative Party will be important in tempering the more extreme monetarists and free-marketeers in the Conservative Government. They may well fear that if the resentment of the disadvantaged is allowed to grow, the result could be political instability and an increase in crime and violence.

Such a holding operation is not enough, however. In the longer term the aim must be for improvement. Two forces have worked against the elimination of poverty – public opinion and the powerlessness of the poor. Hostility and indifference to the poor are unfortunately not new, but are attitudes deeply entrenched in our culture. The solution is not easy to see. To begin to discuss this problem, it should be recognised from the start that poverty is a *moral* problem. The technical and political obstacles to resolving the distinction between the 'deserving' and the 'undeserving' are compounded by differences of values.

Very few would not have compassion for the 'deserving'. The old, the sick, the blind, the disabled arouse feelings of sympathy and altruistic reactions. The main groups suffering from the label 'undeserving poor' are the children in families where either there is only one parent or the father is out of work. But the sins of the fathers are visited on the children still. Two recent cases, both from the North of England, will serve. Four children died in a council house when an irate neighbour pushed burning rags through the letter box and set fire to the house. He/she had been goaded to this by a long-running vendetta between that family and the rest of the estate. The parents both had problems – one was mentally ill, the other a prisoner. Three children died in a fire at a house in Sunderland while their parents were out at a pub. The electricity and gas in the house had been cut off all through the winter, presumably for bad debts, and the house had been lit by candles.

No childhood occurs more than once . . . Any economic doctrine which professes to sell national salvation by scarring the irreplaceable lives of half our people is a fraud before it begins. (*New Statesman* 26 October 1979)

A sense of communal responsibility for children, the sick, the old and for the unemployed will have to be promoted if public opinion is to change. The concern for social justice should include the desire to alter the conditions of life in modern Britain which produce the egoism and escapism that characterize it at present. In the 1940s a mood of popular radicalism existed. Surely we do not need to summon a war to revive those feelings? Forces which contributed importantly to that mood were the social investigations of the 1930s; the political strength of the trade unions and Labour Party;

and a growing awareness of alternatives, developed partly through the education programmes of the armed services. These indicate the contribution that could be made to shifting public opinion by education, broadly defined, especially where this could offer an alternative to the perspective disseminated by the gutter Press.

The resilience of hostility to the unemployed should never be underestimated. In the 1931 election a key issue was that of unemployment insurance; the National Government was bent on economizing, the Labour Party was seen in popular account as having vastly increased unemployment insurance expenditure and Labour suffered a humiliating defeat. In 1959, Labour's promotion of social justice lost out to the campaign of 'you've never had it so good'. Immediate and vivid fears of popular violence have promoted social reform more often than a mood of altruism. Civil servants have moved ahead of public opinion in developing social policies, mainly with an eye to political and social stability but also influenced by liberal and professional concern for equity. The better-off worker has not been keen to support his higher-risk brothers and sisters. The legislation of the 1940s, with its universalistic principle, specifically provided support for the unemployed through the State, at that time, therefore, mainly through the middle-class taxpayer, rather than from the contributions of the better-off worker. As these latter have increasingly been dragged into the tax-net, their traditional resistance to supporting the long-term unemployed, as opposed to the cyclically unemployed, has resurfaced. With the exception of the Beveridge Report, the TUC has rarely played a creative part in the development of social policies. More tolerance of the unemployed may grow as structural unemployment affects those previously protected from such risks. Policies for unemployment would probably also attract more support if they were based not simply on paying out 'dole' but involved imaginative schemes for job creation and work-sharing.

The powerlessness of the poor mirrors their exclusion from the political system, particularly since the Labour Party, their traditional ally, shifted its concern from social justice to economic management. This neglect turned into an attack on the poor as the Party support at the local level declined and pressures from below were reduced.

Social reformism in post-war years has been mainly concerned with two objectives: first, the elimination of poverty; second, the reduction of inequality. This has been simply a continuance of the traditional pursuits of socialism. What successes have been enjoyed by social reformers have resulted from the exercise of persuasion, putting pressure on a system of patronage. As the Welfare State has grown, those who dispense the resources of the State have grown in power. Civil servants and politicians act as patrons to the clients of the Welfare State and grant favours to chosen representatives of these clients. The result is not entirely arbitrary. The force of reason has at times prevailed. At others, however, bending to 'public opinion', the winning of votes or ties of past friendship or shared interest have been more important. Civil servants, with their interest in the efficient managing of the State machine, have been a relatively progressive force and in devising policies they have been influenced by experts in social administration who share their concern for efficiency and fairness. The main changes in social provision in post-war years reflect the adaptation of the system to changing social conditions. In this way, some groups in society have been protected from the worst effects of social changes outside their control. A slight shift has occurred in the relative distribution of favours among those dependent on the State. The old have gained a little ground by vigorously and vociferously organizing in their own interest, aided by a few powerful figures like Jack Jones and the fact that they could be used as a token symbol of social concern at election times. The unemployed have lost ground in the face of the ideological campaign against 'scroungers' conducted by politicians and sections of the Press which has reflected an attempt to justify rising rates of unemployment and concentration of effort on cutting public expenditure since 1976. Families and children have lost out compared to the childless and the single. But these are relatively minor changes within the overall picture which is that, in spite of economic growth and an increase in the standard of living, the relative position of the poor has not improved and poverty remains. Now that we live in a period of nil growth and possible reduction in the standard of living, the immediate prospects for improving the situation of the poor are even worse. If altruism and a concern for equality were not in evidence in the days of affluence and rising expectations, what chance is there that these issues will figure largely in people's minds now?

The new initiatives for reform have come from the Right. Advocating return to a market economy, their themes in social policy are cutting costs, limiting State intervention, promoting economic growth through incentives and the acceptance of inadequacy and scarcity as a fact of life in the social services. The Welfare State may continue at a minimal level, to pick up the pieces, protecting the very weak, but the rest will have to go it alone.

It is true that the extension of means-tested benefits, especially FIS, by an earlier Conservative Government improved the situation of the very poor. Sir Keith Joseph was acclaimed at the Conservative Party Conference when he listed six new social security benefits. But this act of paternalism is at odds with *laissez faire* ideas and is unlikely to be repeated. The pace is now set by policies designed to cut public expenditure and promote economic growth through encouragement of private enterprise. If these strategies prove ineffective, however, the need for alternative proposals will be all the more urgent.

The programme most often offered as an alternative to those which place economic growth prior to social reform emphasises the need for a redistribution of income, wealth and power. Poverty cannot be eradicated nor welfare promoted within the existing system:

Britain consists of a stratified society within which ... income, wealth and power, are unequally divided. Poverty functions to service and justify these divisions. The existence of the poor, who are held responsible for their poverty, implies that the position of the more affluent should be left unchallenged ... the socially deprived provide society with a pool of workers who have no choice but to undertake the ... most unattractive occupations. ... Poverty is thus essential to maintaining the present shape of society. (Holman 1978: 238)

Some have seen the major obstacle to redistribution as lying with 'the affluent worker', the trade unions' protection of differentials and resistance to incomes policy:

For an effective attack to be made on the ugly pools of poverty and social squalor that still exist in this country, the affluent worker as well as the middle class will have to pay for it in higher taxes or disproportionate income restraint or both ... and this is the greatest challenge which the Labour Party now faces. (Marquand 1975)

The implication of this view is that all that is needed is moral leadership and political will which will bind together a refurbished consensus at the centre. R.H. Tawney, the economic historian, however, looked forward to a society in which democracy would mean not merely a 'political system and nothing more ... a form of Government', but also a type of society. This could be achieved by advancing simultaneously on two fronts:

In the first place, the resolute elimination of all forms of special privilege, which favour some groups and depress others, whether their sources be differences of environment, of education, or of pecuniary income . . . in the second place, the conversion of economic power, now often an irresponsible tyrant, into the servant of society, working within clearly defined limits, and accountable for its action to a public authority. (Preface to 1938 edition of *Equality*)

The key issue is that of the connection between poverty and inequality. It could be argued that in a relatively rich society there is no just cause why poverty should remain. There are sufficient resources available to solve the problem of poverty, if redistributed. A concentration of effort on locating those in poverty and directing resources, particularly in the form of cash, towards them is all that is needed. This could be done without considering the causes of poverty. A simple test of means or need would be all that would be required. Poverty may be endemic in society: some are dependent because they are not fit to work; some because no-one wishes to purchase their labour; and others because they do not want to offer their labour for sale. It might be desirable at the same time to attack these causes at root but, so long as poverty remains, the main question should be the technical one of how to direct money efficiently to those who have inadequate incomes. Those who wish to see poverty eliminated from our society should concentrate on putting across the case for a minimum income as of right in or out of work. This effort should not be diluted and confused with quite separate egalitarian aims.

Let us consider as an example what would be the likely effects of the introduction of adequate incomes for those on social security. The most obvious contradiction that would be displayed would be one with which we are quite familiar – the so called poverty trap – that those receiving social security would be better off than those with low pay from employment. Supposing there were a tide running in favour of progressive social reform, the next step would be the improvement of the incomes of the low-paid, either through some kind of income supplement from the State or by effective regulation of wages through wages councils and inspectors. If this were effective, it would then highlight a contrast between the incomes of the erstwhile low-paid and those of skilled workers and others in stable, highly productive employment. The thorny question of differentials would thus have to be faced and its solution would lie in reaching agreement on a fair and just incomes policy. It is obvious that this would not prove acceptable unless it also covered incomes in the form of salaries as well as wages and adequately covered remuneration in the form not only of cash but the whole range of 'fringe benefits', cheap loans, cars, lunches, travelling expenses, pension rights, sickness benefits and so on. Intervention at this level would involve not only control of incomes from employment but also from profits and rent and would raise the question of the right and power of the State to control these resources. Thus, from the apparently simple attempt to provide a minimum income would develop a domino effect which would throw into question the very structure of society.

In fact, if it were quite so simple, it would be difficult to explain why the matter had not been solved by now. Beveridge's proposals were based on just these assumptions. They were framed cogently and clearly and worked out in painstaking detail. If put into practice, as has been frequently pointed out, much of the poverty that remains today would disappear. But, as we saw, his proposals met stiff resistance and were never fully implemented His basic principles were not accepted and the remaining problems which he raised as matters for discussion were never taken up. And that was in the forties when conditions were singularly conducive to social reform. At the present time, when conditions are less favourable, the proposal 'Back to Beveridge' is very unlikely to gain ground. The elimination of poverty is not a technical question but a political one. Its solution depends not only on blueprints but on the balance of political forces and political will.

Recognising that poverty and inequality are inextricably intertwined, leading experts on poverty have concluded that more radical solutions are required. Kincaid believes that: 'The social-democratic programme of accepting capitalist society in all essentials, while attempting to modify it by moderate and gradual reforms, is becoming increasingly unrealistic as a practical political strategy.' (Kincaid 1973: 237) 'Poverty cannot be abolished within capitalist society, but only in a socialist society, under workers' control, in which human needs, and not profits, determine the allocation of resources.' (op. cit.: 247)

Peter Townsend concludes his monumental study of *Poverty in the United Kingdom* (1979) with a discussion of the principles of policy. The direction of social policy, he says, particularly since the late sixties and seventies, has been to the provision of conditional welfare for the few. A second possible principle of provision is that of minimum rights for the many. Taking up the point that this was the cardinal principle of Beveridge's plan, he comments:

In over thirty years since the national insurance scheme was enacted this principle has never been fulfilled. Governments have shrunk from fulfilling it, perhaps because of the implications for public expenditure, but more likely because of the threat that would be posed to the lower reaches of the wage system, and more generally to the kind of employment system appropriate to a capitalist or even a 'mixed' economy. The 1834 Poor Law Commission's principle of less eligibility lives on in the definition of levels and conditions of social security benefits. (:923)

In a footnote, Townsend quotes from the Poor Law Commission to show how little thought has changed:

the first and most essential of all conditions, a principle which we find universally admitted, even by those whose practice is at variance with it, is that (the pauper's) situation on the whole shall not be made really or apparently so eligible as the situation of the independent labourer of the lowest class. (:923)

Townsend recognises that there is 'an in-built tension, and even contradiction, in the application of the principle of a national minimum to a market economy' (op. cit.: 924). His final conclusion is that a third principle should be the basis of social policy – distributional justice for all: an effective assault on poverty would have to include abolition of excessive wealth; abolition of excessive income; introduction of an equitable income structure and some breaking down of the distinction between earners and dependents; abolition of unemployment; reorganisation of employment and professional practice; and the reorganisation of community service. The very last words of his book are:

It would be wrong to suggest that any of this is easy or even likely. The citadels of wealth and privilege are deeply entrenched and have shown tenacious capacity to withstand assaults, notwithstanding the gentleness of their legal, as distinct from the ferocity of their verbal, form. Yet we have observed the elaborate hierarchy of wealth and esteem of which poverty is an integral part. If any conclusion deserves to be picked out from this report as its central message it is this, with which, some time, the British people must come to terms. (:926)

Surely, however, by now we should see that awful warnings and exhortations alone will not be enough to bring about changes. Most of those who criticise the present system place their faith in socialism as the alternative to capitalism. The fate of the poor depends therefore on the prospects for socialism. But there is much confusion as to the meaning of socialism. For too long it has been taken for granted that socialism is a self-explanatory term for a system of social and economic organisation which could be imposed on modern society without too much difficulty given the political will. That it is indeed the most appropriate alternative to capitalism. The variety of socialism referred to in most of the writings which have been touched on in this book rests on concepts of equality, social justice, fraternity and compassion, the moral values that give it coherence and distinguish it from other philosophies. It is too easily assumed that these are the innate and traditional values of the working class: that if the power of the working class could be increased, there would be an almost automatic increase in the extent to which these values would permeate the social order, would act as the principles guiding social and economic organisation. But there is no necessary relationship between the working class and these values. Where justice and equality have been unifying themes, this has more often been to promote solidarity in the face of hardship and oppression. I am not arguing that such conditions have gone for good. But it cannot be easily assumed that the class structure provides a fertile ground for those values. The reports of Goldthorpe and Halsey describe significant changes which have occurred in the social structure of Britain. Particularly important has been the way in which the experience of social mobility has affected class-consciousness. The picture of society which Townsend's book provides is of one divided *hierarchically*. Three rough divisions can be discerned: at the top, the privileged upper groups, comprising the wealthy, professional and managerial sections (what Goldthorpe, following Dahrendorf, calls the service class); a middle section, mainly organised, relatively secure labour; and a third group which could be called the underclass, who are the low-paid, the unemployed and dependent sections of society, the poor. The point is that there seems to be no necessary connection between the interests of the strong groups within this structure and changes which would ensure the dominance of the moral values emphasised by those who promote the causes of justice, equality and compassion for the poor.

As we have seen, reforms cannot be viewed solely as technical matters: the way in which reforms are put into practice and the character they assume reflects the context in which they take place. Nationalisation and council housing are obvious examples of reforms which have not automatically entailed the implementation of socialist principles. Their effect has been rather to reduce support for socialism in those most closely affected. A major effect of the reforms of the post-war years was the creation of the illusion that a Welfare State had been established, that nothing more needed to be done. This led to the dominance of revisionism within the Labour Party and a critical loss of leadership for the socialist movement. Compromise and a loss of independence of thought and action was the result.

There is now much talk in the poverty lobby about its strategy. Fabian tactics of persuasion and advocacy are acknowledged to have had only limited success. Recognising the central importance of the trade unions in the political battle, voices are heard urging the pressure groups to join forces with the trade unions to win support for their campaigns. But why should the trade unions support the poor? What would they gain from such an alliance? In the short term, in the effort to dislodge the Government from its all-out attack on wages, to divert it from its free market tactics, by encouraging a U-turn or even unseating the Conservatives and replacing them with a Labour Government, the support of others suffering from the effects of their policies would be seen as useful. But beyond this, there are few grounds for supposing that the trade unions will promote the interests of the poor. It is naively optimistic to hope for the patronage of the organised labour movement for, unless the poor have something to offer in return for such an alliance, the crumbs of patronage are the most that would be gained.

The split between the respectable and the rough has a long history. Ideas of the deserving and the undeserving will not be transformed overnight, and these categories are not entirely mythical: there are cultural differences between some of the poor and the more affluent workers. To win acceptance by the trade union movement a shift would be required from the poor themselves, who would need to move towards accepting the values of thrift, respectability and discipline that distinguish the former group. The harsh fact that the movement cannot be only in one direction should not be denied or neglected. However, in saying this, it is also apparent that there are other features of the poor which cannot be changed – illness, intelligence, disability, race and sex for example. For a common purpose to arise and for cooperation to be furthered, a change of attitude would be needed on the part of trade unionists, who have not always been particularly distinguished by liberal or progressive attitudes on such matters. Persuasion, education and a moral campaign for socialist values could possibly make some inroads.

A distinctive feature of socialist ideas compared to those of Conservatives is, however, an optimism about human nature. And one does not need to look far to see that concern for those in distress and a willingness to help are still prominent features of our society. Where people are brought into contact with such situations and given the responsibility and opportunity to help, they do respond in ways which support the hope that such reactions could be cultivated and encouraged.

A problem for those who aim to promote concern for social issues is that the poor and other sections of the working class are now geographically separated more markedly than in pre-war days. The poor are concentrated in certain regions, neighbourhoods and work places. Although this is not sufficient to justify area policies to combat poverty, the resulting lack of contact between the poor and others works against the forging of alliances on the basis of common experience. The increased social mobility of post-war years and the flight to the suburbs have been among the factors reducing awareness of social problems among voters. An important motivation of many of those who joined the Labour Party before the war was a concern with the poverty and distress which they saw around them. They saw children without shoes or enough to eat. They saw the unemployed on the street corners. They were often not themselves in poverty or distress. It was compassion for others which urged them to become involved in politics. The continuing trend towards the standardisation of work and the split between the North and the South also separate people in their experience and knowledge of deprivation. Risks are not evenly distributed in society and some are made much more aware than others of the effects of unemployment, sickness, old age, broken homes and so on.

It is noteworthy that the period which has seen a lessening of concern for social reform in political life has also been one in which there has been a vast drop in the numbers who take out individual membership of a political party. I do not believe the concern for social justice has diminished as much as the feeling has grown that social causes cannot be promoted through the political parties. A disenchantment partly with the political parties as vehicles for social reform and even with the political process itself is much in evidence. Private troubles are not translated into public issues. The desire to help is channelled through individual acts of generosity or through taking up professional 'caring' roles, both of which are necessarily limited in effectiveness. The failure of the Labour Party to tap these sources of concern and channel them into effective action must bear a large part of the blame for this.

A prime objective for the poverty lobby should therefore be to encourage all developments which lead to people getting together on the basis of common interests, particularly at the local level, in community organisations and especially at the grass-roots level of the trade unions and the Labour Party. At the same time the leadership of these movements should be encouraged to lead, to set an example and not bow too easily to a 'public opinion' created largely by the Press. The policies promoted should be those which would lead to a redistribution of resources at every level and in every sector of society. The fact that the implementation of any of these will immediately produce paradoxes, contradictions and conflicts should not be taken as a reason to oppose such reforms. It is only through the highlighting of such contradictions, the encouragement of comparisons, that the issues will be recognised and the balance of political forces disturbed and rearranged.

There remains nonetheless the problem of the lack of any immediately apparent shared interests particularly in a period of 'restraint'. However much might be gained by encouraging popular sentiments of compassion and social concern, in the end the poor must act for themselves; they must not place their faith in others. But it is difficult to see how the poor can act in their own interest given all that has been said about their frailty and lack of organisation. Fragmented, weak, powerless and vulnerable, what chances are there for an increase in their political strength?

The most likely area in which successful action in their own interest could be developed is that of the unions of the low-paid workers. It is only through organisation and unionisation that the low-paid can improve their relative position. The immediate objective in the present circumstances would best be to criticise and aim to alter the distribution of resources within their particular sector of industry or services. Tactics are difficult here where campaigns of disruption can easily backfire in a loss of support and respect. In these conditions, the lower paid must work with those just above them in the pay hierarchy, like the lower professionals, nurses, teachers and social workers or clerical and administrative workers. They must develop thoughtful and rational criticisms of the distribution of resources and propose cogent alternatives. This is an area in which social scientists could contribute, offering their skills of research and analysis to the members of these movements. These unions should pursue interests shared with other workers rather than acting alone when they are more likely to be defeated. In this way they will gain strength, allies and experience. But it must be recognised that disruption has often been the way in which the poor have made themselves felt. It should be made plain to the privileged that the leaders can contain the dissatisfactions of their members only so long as some concessions are granted. The tension is between organised disruption, which will lead to real gains and forge alliances with other sections of the labour movement, and disorganised disruption which in creating fear in other groups may lead to a temporary improvement in the situation but later to repression.

The key question in any discussion of the politics of poverty is whether the poor form a distinct social group. If the poor are not a separate class but simply a social category, it would be possible to promote their cause on the basis of interests shared with other groups. Specific alliances could be established on the strength of these shared interests. The poor would offer their weight in votes and voices in political negotiations. Action on specific issues which are also the concern of wider groups would, if successful, give immediate help to the poor. In the process of pursuing such specific campaigns, cooperation would be built up between different sections of the working class and the direct involvement of the poor in political action would help to overcome the isolation and sense of powerlessness which lies at the root of their situation. An example here is the rallies of the Anti-Nazi League which brought together, on the streets and in public parks, members of immigrant workers groups, popular musicians and their followers, young unemployed (especially black) youths and others who until then had had little experience of involvement in British political life or the experience of cooperating with other groups in society. Issues like that of the protection and furtherance of the child benefit scheme could be the focus for common action by a family lobby. Successful pressure to promote women's rights directly aids the poor. The issues of unemployment and regional development are also ones in which there is a common interest among different sections of the working class. Similarly the protection of the health, education and social services is a shared interest. Policies to be promoted are those which would improve conditions for women, for families, for the sick, for employees, for school-leavers, the unemployed, those in the North, Scotland, Northern Ireland and other deprived regions.

Optimism for a strategy of alliances rests on the conclusion that the poor are not a clearly separated caste in society with distinctively different interests and habits. Although there are obviously tendencies encouraging an increase in the dependent sections of the population and in the proportion rejected by the labour market, this process has not produced a permanent class of paupers or a dual labour market. The distinctions refer more to statistical categories than to distinct groups. People on the streets, on estates, in neighbourhoods, at work and school mix together in broad class groupings.

Townsend's emphasis on the *hierarchy* of disadvantage is critical here. Where there is a hierarchy, the possibilities for alliances appear. Social policy should therefore be concerned with services which meet adequately the needs of all children, the sick, the old or the unemployed, not just those at the head of the queue. The better-off and worse-off within the working class have interests in common which unite the securely employed, the low-paid and the unemployed. Bringing up a family, running the risks of disablement and sickness, growing old, these are shared experiences. Only when all people share social services in common and use them on the same terms will the gap between the privileged and the deprived be reduced. The fact that poverty is experienced by large numbers in society at some time in their lives and that even more are aware of deprivation in certain areas of their environment, shows the possibility of action to promote shared interests. The risks of poverty or a relative decline in income in old age or when bringing up children are commonly shared, although greater for some than others. The risks of ill health, also, although concentrated among certain groups, are ones with which everyone has to come to terms. The problems of young people in finding a job or of young couples in finding somewhere to live unite people across the barriers of region, race and sex. Poor schools and poor hospitals are experienced by a range of people living in a particular area who are not all 'the bottom 10 per cent' or the low-paid or claimants. The complexity of social life is the ground on which a strategy of alliances rests.

Many developments in post-war years, however, as we have seen, have served to widen the divisions between people: selective services for the poor and the poorest, provided by the State; select services for the better-off, provided by private insurance arranged either individually or increasingly through negotiation between managers and employees. To overcome such divisions and revive the values of fraternity and compassion will be a gigantic task. The last point to stress is that action in any one area alone will be ineffective for it will always end up by robbing Peter to pay Paul: pressure has to be evenly exerted in all areas and at every level. To outlaw the politics of dog eat dog, firm leadership is needed to organise a concerted campaign for social reform. And here the Labour Party must again be seen to play the key part in relating these separate activities into an uncompromising programme of reform.

The persistence of inequalities in Britain and particularly the division between the 'two nations', one secure, affluent and comfortable, the other bearing a greater share of the 'diswelfares' of industrial society, is the product of indifference, ignorance and a lack of political commitment to change. The affluence and comfort of the one sector is at the expense of the other, the bottom fifth of the work force, who do the menial and unskilled jobs; the residents of overspill estates and tower blocks; of the inner-city areas; the 3 million unemployed; those on hospital waiting-lists; the 5 million dependent on supplementary benefit; and the further 5 million living at or just above this level. The Labour Party and the trade unions must bear the main responsibility for the seizing-up of the motor of social reform. A party of reform should aim to inform and educate, to heighten awareness of problems and the changes required to solve them. The Labour Party, by allowing 'public opinion' to dictate its priorities, in the desire to win favour with the electorate, let slip the initiative for change. This is not simply a case of 'betrayal by the leadership'. The main problem has been one of lack of contact between representatives of the Labour movement and working people at the grass roots, contact which would allow a flow of ideas and attitudes in both directions, representation and education.

The Labour Party has slipped away from the people. It has become increasingly elitist and divorced from the grass roots. A great deal of work needs to be done to transform it into a socialist party, a real alternative to either the paternalism of Sir Ian Gilmour or Mrs Thatcher's radical Right rhetoric.

At present the poor are under attack. The continuing support of pressure groups is needed. Immediate alliances can be formed with those employed in the welfare services, whose jobs are similarly threatened. Such alliances and more active grass-roots participation are beginning to make themselves felt. These developments must be supported if we are to resist being dragged further towards the selfish, materialistic jungle which is now cynically sold as our only hope for the future.

BIBLIOGRAPHY

ABEL-SMITH, BRIAN (1958) 'Whose Welfare State' in *Conviction* (ed. N. MACKENZIE), MacGibbon & Kee.

ABEL-SMITH, BRIAN and TOWNSEND, PETER (1965) *The Poor and the Poorest*, Bell.

ABRAMS, MARK and ROSE, RICHARD (1960) *Must Labour Lose?* Penguin. (With a commentary by Rita Hinden)

ATKINSON, A.B. (1972) 'Inequality and social security' in *Labour and Inequality* (eds Peter Townsend and Nicholas Bonsanquet), Fabian Society.

ATKINSON, A.B. (1973) 'Low pay and the cycle of poverty' in *Low Pay* (ed. Frank Field), Arrow Books.

ATKINSON, A.B. (1975) *The Economics of Inequality*, Clarendon Press.

BANTING, K.G. (1979) *Poverty, Politics and Policy: Britain in the 1960s*, Macmillan.

BEER, S.H. (1965) *Modern British Politics: A study of parties and pressure groups*, (2nd edn, Faber and Faber, 1969).

BEVERIDGE, SIR WILLIAM (1942) *Social Insurance and Allied Services: Report by Sir William Beveridge*, Cmnd 6404, HMSO (Nov. 1942) Reprinted 1978.

BEVERIDGE, W. (1953) *Power and Influence*, Hodder & Stoughton.

BOOTH, CHARLES (1903) *Life and Labour of the People in London* (17 vols), Macmillan.

BOSANQUET, NICK and TOWNSEND, PETER (1980) *Labour and Equality: A Fabian study of Labour in power*, Heinemann.

BRAVERMAN, H. (1974) *Labour and Monopoly Capital*, Monthly Review Press.

BRIGGS, ASA (1961) 'The Welfare State in historical perspective' *European Journal of Sociology*, Vol. 2, No. 2, pp. 221–58.

BRUCE, MAURICE (1968) *The Coming of the Welfare State* (4th edn), B.T. Batsford.

BULLOCK, A.L.C. *The Life and Times of Ernest Bevin* (2 vols), Heinemann. Vol. 1, 1960; Vol. 2, 1967.

BUTLER, D.E. and KING, ANTHONY (1965) *The British General Election of 1964*, Macmillan.

BUTLER, D.E. and PINTO-DUSCHINSKY, MICHAEL (1971) *The British General Election of 1970*, Macmillan.

BUTLER, R.A. (1973) *The Art of the Possible*, Penguin.

COATES, KEN and SILBURN, RICHARD (1973) *Poverty: The forgotten Englishmen*, Pelican ed.

COLE, G.D.H. (1942) *Great Britain in the Post-War World*, Victor Gollancz.

COMMISSION OF THE EUROPEAN COMMUNITIES (1977) *The Perception of Poverty in Europe*, March 1977.

CRAIG, F.W.S. (ed.) (1975) *The Most Gracious Speeches to Parliament 1900–1974. Statements of Government Policy and Achievement*, Macmillan.

CROSLAND, C.A.R. (1963) *The Future of Socialism*, Schocken Books, revised edition first published 1957.

CROSSMAN, RICHARD (1969) *Paying for the Social Services*, Fabian Society.

CROSSMAN, RICHARD (1975, 1976, 1977) *The Diaries of a Cabinet Minister* (3 vols), Hamish Hamilton and Jonathan Cape.

DHSS (1977a) *Social Security Research*, Papers presented at a DHSS Seminar on 7–9 April 1976, HMSO 1977.

DHSS (1977b) Supplementary Benefits Commission. *Supplementary Benefits Handbook. A guide to claimants' rights*. Supplementary Benefits Administration Papers 2. Revised Feb. 1977.

DHSS (1978a) Poverty Seminar. 'The distributive share of DHSS expenditure', paper by Economic Adviser's Office. April 1978.

DHSS (1978b) *Social Assistance. A review of the Supplementary Benefits Scheme in Great Britain* July 1978.

FIEGEHEN, G.C. LANSLEY, P.S. and SMITH, A.D. (1977) *Poverty and Progress in Britain, 1953–1973*, National Institute of Economic and Social Research, Occasional Paper XXIX.

FIELD, FRANK and TOWNSEND, PETER (1975) *A Social Contract for Families*, CPAG

FIELD, FRANK (1978) 'The comeback of poverty', *New Statesman*, 29 Sept.

FREUD, DAVID (1978) 'Changing patterns in British employment', *Financial Times*, 28 July.

FRIEDMAN, MILTON (1963) *Capitalism and Freedom*, Univ. of Chicago Press.

FRIEDMAN, MILTON (1980) *Free to Choose*, Pelican.

GALBRAITH, J.K. (1958) *The Affluent Society*, Hamish Hamilton.

GILMOUR, IAN (1978) *Inside Right. A Study of Conservatism*, Quartet Books (first published by Hutchinson & Co., 1977).

GILMOUR, SIR IAN (1980) 'Conservatism'. Lecture delivered at the Cambridge Union, 7 Feb 1980.

GOLDING, PETER and MIDDLETON, SUE (1978) 'Why is the press so obsessed with welfare scroungers?' *New Society*, 26 Oct.

GOLDTHORPE, JOHN in collaboration with C. LLEWELLYN and C. PAYNE, (1980) *Social Mobility and Class Structure in Modern Britain*, OUP.

HABERMAS, JURGEN (1976) *Legitimation Crisis*, Heinemann. (Trans. Thomas McCarthy first published 1973).

HAILSHAM, VISCOUNT (1959) *The Conservative Case*, Penguin.

HALSEY, A.H., HEATH, A.F. and RIDGE, J.M. (1980) *Origins and Destinations*, OUP.

HANCOCK, W.K. and GOWING, M.M. (1949) *British War Economy. History of the Second World War*, UK Civil Series, HMSO.

HARRINGTON, MICHAEL (1962) *The Other America*, Penguin.

HARRIS, JOSÉ (1975) 'Social Planning in war-time: some aspects of the Beveridge Report', in (ed. M. Winter) *War and Economic Development* CUP, pp. 239–55.

HARRIS, R. and SELDON, A. (1979) *Over-Ruled on Welfare*, IEA.

HARVEY, AUDREY (1960) *Casualties of the Welfare State*, Fabian Society.

HAYEK, F.A. (1976) *Law, Legislation and Liberty*. Vol. 11: *The Mirage of Social Justice*, Routledge and Kegan Paul.

HIGGINS, J.M. (1978) *The Poverty Business: Britain and America*, Blackwell, Martin Robertson.

HINDESS, BARRY (1971) *The Decline of Working Class Politics*, MacGibbon & Kee.

HOBSBAWM, E.J. (1968) 'Poverty', in (ed. D.L. Sills) *New International Encyclopaedia of the Social Sciences*, Vol. 12. Macmillan.

HOLMAN, ROBERT (1978) *Poverty: Explanations of Social Deprivation*, Martin Robertson.

HOWE, G. (1961) 'Reform of the Social Services', in (eds L. Beaton *et al.*) *Principles in Practice*, Conservative Political Centre.

JACKSON, DUDLEY (1972) *Poverty*, Macmillan Studies in Economics, Macmillan.

JENKINS, ROY (1959) *The Labour Case*, Penguin.

JOSEPH, SIR KEITH (1972) 'The Cycle of Deprivation'. Speech given at Conference organised by the Pre-School Playgroups Association, 29 June.

KINCAID, J.C. (1973) *Poverty and Equality in Britain. A study of social security and taxation*, Penguin.

LAWSON, NIGEL (1979) 'The Labour Myth about Equality', *Observer*, 15 April.

MACKENZIE, N. (ed.) (1958) *Conviction*, MacGibbon & Kee.

MACLEOD, IAN and POWELL, ENOCH (1952) *The Social Services: Needs and Means*, Conservative Political Centre.

MARQUAND, DAVID (1975) 'The challenge to the Labour Party', *Political Quarterly*, Oct.

MARWICK, ARTHUR (1967) 'The Labour Party and the Welfare State in Britain', *Amer. Hist. Review*, Dec.

MARWICK, ARTHUR (1970) *Britain in the Century of Total War: War, Peace and Social Change 1900–1967*, The Bodley Head, 1968, (Pelican ed., 1970.)

MEACHER, M. (1974) *Scrounging on the Welfare: The Scandal of the Four Week Rule*, Arrow Books.

METCALF, DAVID (1979) 'Shouldering the burden of unemployment', *The Guardian*, 30 July.

MIDDLEMAS, KEITH (1979) *Politics in Industrial Society. The Experience of the British System since 1911*, Andre Deutsch.

MILIBAND, R. (1974) 'Politics and poverty', in *Poverty, Inequality and Class Structure* (ed. Dorothy Wedderburn) CUP.

MORRIS, MARGARET (1978), 'Those we like to help', *New Society* Vol. 53, No. 822, 6 July, p. 18.

NATIONAL BOARD FOR PRICES AND INCOMES (1971) *General Problems of Low Pay*, HMSO, April.

NORTH TYNESIDE, CDP (1978) *In and Out of Work: A study of Unemployment, low pay and income-maintenance services.*

NORTHCOTT, JIM (1964) *Why Labour?*, Penguin Books.

PEACOCK, A. (1961) 'The Welfare Society' in *Unservile State Papers*, Liberal Party.

PIACHAUD, DAVID (1979) *The Cost of a Child*, CPAG.

PLATT, J. (1976) *The Realities of Social Research*, Chatto & Windus.

ROSE, HILARY and JAKUBOWICZ, ANDRE (1978) 'The rise and fall of welfare rights', *New Society*, 1 Sept.

ROWNTREE, SEEBOHM B. (1901) *Poverty: A Study of Town Life*, Macmillan.

ROWNTREE, SEEBOHM and LAVERS, G.R. (1951) *Poverty and the Welfare State*, Longman.

ROYAL COMMISSION ON THE DISTRIBUTION OF INCOME AND WEALTH (1975) *Report No. 1 Initial Report on the Standing Reference*, Cmnd 6171, HMSO July.

SAVILLE, JOHN (1965) 'Labour and income distribution' in *The Socialist Register*, Merlin Press, pp. 151 ff.

SEYD, PAT (1976) 'The child poverty action group', *The Political Quarterly*, Vol. 47.

SIMEY, T.S. and SIMEY, M.B. (1960) *Charles Booth: Social Scientist*, OUP.

SLOOTEN, R. VAN and COVERDALE, A.G. (1977) 'The characteristics of low income households', in *Social Trends* No. 8, HMSO.

STEDMAN JONES, GARETH (1971) *Outcast London: A study in the relationship between classes in Victorian society*, Clarendon Press.

STEWART, MICHAEL (1977) *The Jekyll and Hyde Years: politics and economic policy since 1964*, J.M. Dent.

TAWNEY, R.H. (1964) *Equality*, Unwin Books. (First published 1931.)

TAYLOR, A.J.P. (1978) '1932–1945' in *Coalitions in British Politics*, (ed. D. Butler), Macmillan.

TAYLOR, A.J.P. (1979) 'Alarm in high places', *Observer* 8 April.

THATCHER, MARGARET (1977) *Let Our Children Grow Tall: selected speeches 1975–77*, Centre for Policy Studies.

TITMUSS, RICHARD (1958) *Essays on the Welfare State*, Allen & Unwin.

TITMUSS, RICHARD (1960) *The Irresponsible Society*, Fabian Society.

TITMUSS, RICHARD (1971) *Problems of Social Policy (Civil Histories of the Second World War)*, Greenwood (Reprint of 1st edn HMSO and Longman, 1950.)

TOLAND, SUE (1970) 'Social commentary: changes in living standards since the 1950s', *Social Trends* 10, HMSO.

TOWNSEND, PETER (1954) 'The meaning of poverty', *British Journal of Sociology*, June.

TOWNSEND, PETER (1958) 'A society for people' in *Conviction* (ed. Norman MacKenzie), MacGibbon and Kee, pp. 93–120.

TOWNSEND, PETER (1974) 'The history of a confused thesis' in *BASW National Study Conference on the Cycle of Deprivation*, March.

TOWNSEND, PETER (1976), *Sociology and Social Policy*, Penguin Education. (First published by Allen Lane, 1975.)

TOWNSEND, PETER (1979) *Poverty in the United Kingdom: A study of household resources and standards of living*, Penguin.

The politics of poverty

WALZER, MICHAEL (1971) 'World War II – why was this war different?', *Philosophy and Public Affairs*, Vol. 1, No. 1.

WESTERGAARD, J. and RESLER, H. (1976) *Class in a Capitalist Society: A Study of Contemporary Britain*, Heinemann, 1975. (Pelican 1976.)

WILSON, HARRIET and HERBERT, G.W. (1978) *Parents and Children in the Inner City*, Routledge and Kegan Paul.

WOOTTON, G. (1978) *Pressure Politics in Contemporary Britain*, Lexington Books.

WYNN, M. (1970) *Family Policy*, Michael Joseph.

YOUNG M. (1974) *Poverty Report*, Maurice Temple Smith.

INDEX

Abel-Smith, Brian, 46, 47, 73, 105, 106, 136, 137, 141, 142
academics, 8, 62, 65, 140, 142, 144, 155, 156, 161
Adley, R., 157
advisers, 36, 116, 152–3
Agenda for a Generation, 114
altruism, 87, 107, 119
Anderson, Sir John, 121
anti-welfare backlash, 104
army education, 4
Atkinson, A.B., 117–18
Attlee, Clement, 103

backbench MPs, 4, 12, 21
Banting, K.G., 116
Beer, S.H., 119
Better Pensions, 1974, 34
Bevan, Aneurin, 103, 104
Beveridge, Sir William, 5–21, 23, 36, 41, 66, 67, 76, 99, 121, 138, 145, 172
Beveridge Report, Plan, 6–13, 65, 66, 90, 102, 172
Bevin, Ernest, 7, 15, 103, 122
Birch, Nigel, 126
Booth, Charles, 63–5, 67
Braverman, H., 72
Britain: Progress and Change, 114
Bruce, Maurice, 20
budget, 1980, 40
Butler, R.A., 122, 125, 127
Butskellism, 92

Callaghan, James, 116–17, 144, 149
capital, 74, 79

capital/labour, 78
capitalism, 87
capitalist society, 79
Centre for Policy Studies, 162
centrist view, 89–91
child allowances *see* tax
Child Benefit Act, 35
child benefits, 35, 120, 131, 142–49; *see also* family allowances
Child Poverty Action Group, 35, 116, 117, 118, 129, 135, 137, 138, 140–7
    children in poverty, 35, 46, 48, 51–2, 70–1
    policies for, 6, 10, 35, 146–9
chronic sick, 30, 46; *see also* sick, the
Churchill, Winston, 5, 12, 73, 121, 122
Circumstances of Families, 1966, 147
civil servants, 5, 8, 13, 14, 39, 65, 88, 121, 127, 129, 135, 136, 141, 148, 150–5, 169
claimants, 31, 39–40, 78, 83, 132, 149–50, 157–60
Claimants Unions, 149–50
Clark, Colin, 161
class
    conflict, 78, 91, 166
    consciousness, 73, 77, 98, 114, 118
    structure, 25–6, 77–9
clawback, 116–17, 144
Coalition Government, 5–17
Coates, Ken, 77, 78
Cole, G.D.H., 8
collaboration, 3, 5, 21, 23, 100
collective bargaining, 32, 104, 110, 145
collectivism, 11, 18, 86–9

Index

Index

Index

HOUSING AND SOCIAL JUSTICE
Gill Burke
First published 1981

Housing offers so many different dimensions for discussion. This book provides a basic introduction to housing and housing policy in Britain and examines how the various sectors have developed, the problems these developments have caused and the part policy has played in their change. It looks at the causes and effects of bad housing and housing shortage with particular reference to homelessness, squatting and rural and urban deprivation. The final section evaluates recent housing policy with reference to social justice. The author challenges the role of social policy in achieving a fair distribution of welfare resources. A large section of the book contains documentary material to provide both evidence and stimulation.

The text is aimed at students taking social policy or social work courses at first year undergraduate or diploma level. It can also be used as an introduction for students in other disciplines and on professional courses.

THE ELDERLY IN MODERN SOCIETY
Anthea Tinker
First published 1981

Economic constraints combined with the projected large increase in the numbers of frail elderly pose difficult problems for families and policy makers in the next two or three decades. By taking into account a wide range of literature from medicine, architecture, sociology, psychology and social policy media, this book presents an account of the present situation and analyses some of the problems and options for the future. The author suggests that families and voluntary bodies will have to play an even greater part than they already do in family care and that realistic supportive services are necessary. In contrast it is also noted that many elderly people require little in the way of services and their contribution to society is greatly under-estimated. The book also includes a summary of recent major surveys with views of the effect of recent changes in the organisation of the social services on the elderly.

This text is aimed at students studying degree and diploma courses in social policy. It also presents a reappraisal of society's responsibilities towards the elderly, and will stimulate great interest among social workers, trainee social workers, and the general public.